"Read this exciting book carefully! It will inspire your church to give. It will guide the leadership in your congregation on ways to motivate the people to give more. I know Chester Tolson very well. He was on my staff for twelve years helping me to raise funds for our international ministry. He's not just a theoretical fund-raiser. He knows, firsthand, how to do it. He shares his many years of experience in this book. Whatever the fund-raising needs might be in your church, you will find direction from this book on how to meet those needs. I recommend it for every church or nonprofit institution faced with the challenges of raising funds to support their mission."

—Robert E. Schuller, founder and senior pastor, Crystal Cathedral,
Garden Grove, California

"A timely piece of work filled with great insight, and a must read if our commitment is to keep our community church alive and responsive. Tolson has masterfully revealed to us that stewardship is a vital catalyst for church growth. The solutions that he provides enable the church to aggressively move forward to strengthen its administrative infrastructure by devising and implementing systematic plans predicated on and inspired by the Word of God."

—Dr. Robert J. Brown, chairman and CEO, B&C Associates, Inc.

"Expert and novice fund-raisers alike will benefit from the proven principles shared in this readable volume."

—Ronald L. Ellis, Ph.D., president, California Baptist University

"Drawing from a rich reservoir of experience, Chester Tolson shares with us the most complete and practical presentation on Christian giving I have seen in my thirty-five years of ministry."

—James Capps, senior pastor, Southport Presbyterian Church,
Indianapolis, Indiana

"Chester Tolson is a proven champion who has successfully practiced this book's proven principles for finding funds. This outstanding book is definitely a must read."

—Walt Kallestad, senior minister, Community Church of Joy,
Glendale, Arizona

"This book describes in precise, easy-to-read language the theological principles of giving and the tremendous blessings and rewards that result from biblical stewardship. This step-by-step primer for sound church fiscal planning and management should be required reading for all who seek to maximize the giving potential of one's church."

—Daryl C. Higgins, senior minister, First Protestant Church,
New Braunfels, Texas

"This book is a great balance between biblical teaching and practical approach. Every pastor and church leader should read it. As Chester says, 'Great things don't just happen . . . they all take money.' Consider your effort in reading it an investment that will pay great dividends—literally!"

—Dr. Kent R. Hunter, The Church Doctor, Corunna, Indiana

"The most thorough and practical treatment of financial stewardship I have ever read. These are powerfully positive principles I wish I had learned in preparation for ministry. I know they will strengthen my effectiveness as the chief resource raiser in my congregation."

—Michael Ward, senior pastor, Central United Church, Calgary, Alberta, Canada

"I am constantly faced with finding funds to meet the hopes and needs of my congregation. In this book, Dr. Tolson shares his helpful ideas from many years of fund-raising experiences. It is a guide for all church leaders."

—Father Charles B. Weiser, St. Michael's Roman Catholic Church, West End, New Jersey

"Chester Tolson has 'been there and done that' and understands the issues of funding, budgeting, and numerous other issues facing Christian leaders today. This book will be invaluable in helping local church leaders sort out the issues and options in financing. In addition, Chester writes not only from his practical experience but also from the point of view of a good theologian. I'm sure the reader will find this book an excellent resource."

—Bob Pierson, senior pastor, Christ United Methodist Church, Tulsa, Oklahoma

"In this book, Chester brings the wisdom of God in fund-raising. It worked for him at the Crystal Cathedral and is applicable to every church because it is biblically based."

—Bishop LeRoy Bailey Jr., The First Cathedral, Bloomfield, Connecticut

"How many times have we said, 'If only we had the funds to do that'? I have seen firsthand how Dr. Tolson helps a church move past that question to the more exciting one: 'What now would God have us do with all these blessings?' Church leaders of every kind will find in this book invaluable help in making that leap."

—Rev. Daniel D. Meyer, senior pastor, Christ Church of Oakbrook, Illinois

"Don't buy this book—unless you want to raise a whole lot of money!"

—Jess Moody, pastor, author, and educator

"As the pastor of a growing church, I am always faced with the challenges of raising funds. Chester Tolson is perhaps the most gifted resource person in the church world in the field of funding major projects. As a pastor and spiritual leader in the church, Reverend Chester Tolson approaches fund-raising on a biblical stewardship basis. His book presents a truly 'biblical theology of giving.' This book would have been an extremely valuable tool for me to have years ago, and is one that I will use on a regular basis."

—Rev. Thomas F. Reid, senior pastor, The Tabernacle, Orchard Park, New York

PROVEN PRINCIPLES
for
FINDING FUNDS

*A Guide for Church
and Nonprofit Leaders*

Chester L. Tolson

Baker Books
A Division of Baker Book House Co
Grand Rapids, Michigan 49516

© 2003 by Chester L. Tolson

Published by Baker Books
a division of Baker Book House Company
P.O. Box 6287, Grand Rapids, MI 49516-6287
www.bakerbooks.com

Printed in the United States of America

Library of Congress Cataloging-in-Publication Data

Tolson, Chester, 1923–
      Proven principles for finding funds : a guide for church and non-profit leaders / Chester Tolson.
            p.   cm.
      Includes bibliographical references and index.
      ISBN 0-8010-9148-9 (pbk.)
      1. Church fund raising. I. Title.
BV772.5.T69 2003
254′.8—dc21   2002009511

To my children and grandchildren. From their early years, they loved to share and demonstrated the powerful natural urge to give.

To all the institutions (religious, educational, and social) with which I have worked over the years in helping to raise funds. The positive and far-reaching results of their services have furnished lasting proof of the great good that will come out of our gifts and contributions.

Special thanks to my daughter, Kathy Tolson, who prepared the manuscript for the publisher.

CONTENTS

INTRODUCTION

Money, or the lack of it, is basic to the life, growth, and health of a congregation. With an adequate amount of money, the congregation can pursue its mission. With a lack of money, the programs of the congregation may be stifled, and institutional hardship may result. Addressing the question of money is a prime subject for congregational leadership.

Not only is money vital in keeping the church functioning, but it is also a key subject for the spiritual development of every member of the church's family. In this book we will look at attitudes toward money and how people handle it in their own individual lives. The Bible and church history are clear on this question of stewardship. We are instructed to earn all we can and save all we can in order to give all we can. This axiom is not a negative requirement but a blessing. God gives the increase, but we are the instruments to make it happen. Church fund-raising must start on this high spiritual level.

When the publisher invited me to write this book, we decided to focus primarily on fund-raising in the church. The church has unique needs, challenges, opportunities, and methods associated with raising money that separate it from other institutions. However, much of the material in this book also will help other institutions that need to appeal for funds to support their programs. This is especially true in the chapters about:

- why people give (chapter 2)
- capital funding (chapter 7)
- deferred giving (chapter 8)
- endowments (chapter 9)

This book is not intended as a "do it yourself" handbook. One reason I resisted writing a book on fundraising was because I knew it was more complex and sophisticated than merely writing a recipe that would always work. Needs vary, people vary, and institutions vary. Raising funds successfully requires specific attention to individual situations and needs. However, any group may study these time-proven principles and make great progress. In many instances a church may need the experience of professional counsel to make fundraising happen more quickly and more successfully. This book will examine the role of the professional fundraiser. Yet any church anywhere may take these principles, with or without professional counsel, and make enormous strides in developing a stewardship-driven church. Read the "how to" steps carefully. Set up a program to implement them. Start now. Work on the themes in this book constantly. Don't give up. Know that you can raise money in your church to meet your needs. This book will help you.

The ideas, suggestions, and methods presented here have been used successfully in my own experience. Out of respect for donor privacy, I have omitted names and personal references.

For nearly forty years, I have worked full time in raising funds for institutions seeking charitable gifts, including:

- colleges and universities
- professional schools
- private secondary schools
- parish churches

I also guided groups of parish churches seeking funds together for such denominational causes as:

- paracongregation ministries
- health care institutions
- social causes
- community projects
- arts and cultural institutions

Through all of these various appeals for diverse causes, I have used many of the same proven principles that work. In this book I will share these principles in the hope that they may strengthen your ability to raise funds needed for your important ministries. *purpose of book*

I did not set out to be a fund-raiser. In college I received a call for ministry. I graduated from a theological seminary and accepted a call as the pastor of a congregation. It wasn't long before I was exposed to the need for raising funds.

From that parish job, I became an executive for the presbytery of Los Angeles. During this time in the mid-fifties, new churches were springing up all over southern California. Most of my daily schedule involved getting churches organized, securing property, assisting in getting buildings erected, and creating programs that would attract the people in the communities. Everything required money. I became a fund-raiser.

From there I established a brand-new congregation in a community that had no church. We needed to purchase land, underwrite a program, and build a church building. I was a fund-raiser.

In the mid-sixties, my denomination undertook a national capital fund-raising campaign to raise funds for its schools, new church development, social causes, church-sponsored medical centers, and mission work around the world. It was called the "Fifty-Million Fund." Our goal was to raise that amount of money to help underwrite the capital needs. I was invited to help and became an area director for the campaign. We exceeded our goal. I liked fund-raising.

When that campaign was over, my job assignment terminated. I went to Trinity University, a Presbyterian university in San Antonio, Texas, as a development officer. It was the school's centennial year, which meant I was very busy being a fund-raiser. At the end of the year, I accepted an invitation from Ketchum, Inc., then the largest and oldest professional fund-raising group, to become a director in the firm. I was assigned to direct enormous capital campaigns for several major universities. This fund-raising experience was invaluable.

In 1970 I organized my own fund-raising firm, C. L. Tolson and Associates. We conducted capital campaigns and offered professional fund-raising counsel for diverse institutions. In 1985 I accepted an invitation from Dr. Robert Schuller at the Crystal Cathedral to conduct a one-year campaign to raise funds for a family life center. When that campaign was over, I stayed on for nearly twelve more years raising funds for capital needs, endowment funds, and the annual church budget appeal. These were years of productive service. Whether I initially intended it or not, I am a fund-raiser and have been most of my adult life.

I remain active in fund-raising counsel and help direct capital funds campaigns each year as requested. In addition I have a real passion for helping to create senior housing on church campuses and work with a national group to develop these projects.

This has been the trail I have traveled. I've learned some things on the journey and am pleased to share them with you. I truly hope this book will be helpful and meaningful for you.

1

WHAT MAKES PEOPLE GIVE?

Giving starts in the heart, moves into the brain, and then reaches out with an open hand. The giving cycle starts with the impulse to do something good for someone or something beyond ourselves. We have an urge to share. This is an emotional characteristic. Our feelings are activated through information, direction, and persuasion. The brain takes the emotional urge and turns it into action to fill a need. Fund-raising recognizes these basic stages of giving and creates the environment for the prospective donor to give to a specific cause.

Giving Is Natural

We have within us a natural desire to give. We see examples of this all the time. On the morning of September 11, 2001, our nation was violated by terrorists.

This dastardly attack on our own land was a national tragedy like we had never experienced before. We were shocked, angry, and motivated to bring the perpetrators to deserving justice. Before nightfall people's natural giving desire began. Rescue workers gave their own lives in their attempt to bring others to safety. Many people of all colors, traditions, and religious and political allegiances rushed to blood banks to give their blood to support others in their battle to survive. Food, clothing, supplies, money, and services came from all sections of our nation and beyond. We were all moved by this natural impulse to give. People everywhere were saying, "What can I do?" "How can I give?" This national tragedy brought out their desire to give.

I serve as the director of Churches Uniting in Global Mission (CUGM). This is a national network of ministers from across all denominational lines, representing churches in all areas of our nation. They share one common trait: they are the senior pastors of many of the largest congregations in America, including all the traditional Protestant denominations, charismatic and independent churches, and Roman Catholic and Orthodox churches. Many of them told me the same story in the days immediately following this national disaster. All of their congregations were overflowing at every service. "The attendance was so large that it looked like Easter, but it wasn't an Easter crowd." Many in the congregations "were not church people at all." One pastor of a large Midwestern congregation told me about a middle-aged woman who stopped him after the worship service and said that she had never before been inside a church. He asked her why she was there, and she said that she wanted to do something to help.

The cynic might say that she was motivated by fear to attend church. If so, that wasn't such a bad idea, because we are taught that "perfect love casts out fear," and she could get in touch with that love in church. So much for the cynic. She told the pastor she was there because she wanted to do something to help. She was seeking to give. Giving is a natural human response, and the church should appeal to that natural desire by pointing to opportunities to give to its mission.

One of my fund-raising clients during this national disaster was Metro Ministries in New York, with its founding pastor, Bill Wilson. There may be nothing like this ministry anywhere else. It has the largest Sunday school in the nation. Each week over twenty thousand kids living in the roughest environment of the inner city are picked up from the tenements and bused to locations for a Christian message of hope. In some areas trucks outfitted with stage and PA systems go to fifty-six sites for services in New York's most crisis-ridden neighborhoods, teaching love, forgiveness, and purpose. Metro Ministries has been doing this for over twenty years. Now over 60 percent of their current staff and workers grew up riding buses to these "sidewalk Sunday schools."

Many people in their church family were living in the shadows of "ground zero" where the major disaster occurred. These families turned to Metro Ministries for food, shelter, and spiritual counsel. In the days immediately after the tragic event, Bill Wilson called me to say that people from everywhere were asking, "What can we do?" This is a natural human response. The church should be available with its message and needs to provide people the opportunity to give.

This natural desire to give evidences itself early in life. I saw it in my children; I see it demonstrated daily in my grandchildren, who appear to be the happiest when they are giving and sharing. I experienced this in my own life. I grew up in Los Angeles during the depression years. None of us had much money. As people of that generation have said, "We were really poor, but we didn't know it." As a very young boy at Christmas season, I would go from door to door, selling some simple trinkets. I wanted to earn money to buy each member of my family a Christmas gift. I was driven by the natural urge to give. As you look back over your early life, you probably can confirm this desire to share.

This desire to give may drive much of our life's behavior. Giving should really be at the top of our spending list. The church should make this giving urge a fundamental foundation for discipleship and Christian living.

People Give out of Tradition, Peer Pressure, and Environment

Some people are strongly motivated to give because of a family tradition for philanthropy. This is especially true of those wealthier families who have an established philanthropic image to uphold. The church should recognize this motivation "button" and push it when appropriate. For example, this factor for giving becomes especially relevant when a church is seeking gifts beyond the regular annual support appeal, such as for a building fund campaign. People who are not regularly involved in the congregation's life may respond to a special appeal because of the family's past connection to the church. They are driven by this family tradition. This reason for giving is often at the source of major gifts. I have seen this happen often. Moreover I have seen these same people, who seldom attend the church or appear to have little interest in it, become regular attenders and supporters of the church after giving to a special project, perhaps because they want to protect their investment. Giving, therefore, can be a strong evangelistic instrument. The gift, motivated by the urge to fulfill the family tradition, may be the catalyst for relighting the Christian faith. Churches must always be on the alert for these opportunities.

Some people are motivated to give out of peer pressure. This motivation often arises from the examples that other friends and church members have set. Churches that are successful in raising funds see that motivation factor often and create a fellowship environment for this to happen. Established groups such as women's and men's organizations, couples' groups, volunteer and study groups fall into these natural areas for gifting. The rise of small fellowship groups or cells, often referred to as "covenant groups," may become a motivating agent in developing gifts through this "holy peer pressure." Of course that is not the primary purpose for fellowship groups, but it is a natural fallout of the congregation gathering in smaller segments. It creates a "win-win" situation. Through the fellowship of the smaller groups, the church raises more funds for its general mission; and through the giving of the funds, the members of the smaller fellowship grow in their own Christian faith. The church should recognize this peer giving motivation as good and viable in establishing its fund-raising strategies.

The environment of the institution has a lot to do with motivating gifts and support. If the congregation is a joyous, upbeat, and happy group, the giving will reflect positively. If the church is self-serving, divided, and downbeat, the giving results will be negative. You cannot raise funds on the tune of a minor chord. It takes a major chord to get the giving faucet to flow. I have worked with churches where the atmosphere is alive and expectant. Those churches were successful in raising the funds to service an exciting and growing mission. I have worked with churches where the environment was dead and doubting, and the fund-raising results were dismal. Walt Kallestad, in his book *Turn Your Church Inside Out,* pointed out that the secret of creating this positive environment is to "build a church for others."[1]

In this same context, a congregation must create the environment for giving by being a giving church. Statistics show that churches that place greater emphasis on mission dollars going outside the congregation raise more money for their own local mission. I've worked for several churches that moved from financial depression to financial success when they deliberately gave more money away. How can you expect individual church members to respond to the call to give if the church making the call is miserly in its support for the larger mission of the church? Challenge your church to try this. I have not heard of a church that sincerely tried this approach and didn't reap great results. They continued to be a giving church not only because it was the right thing to do but also because it was the wise thing to do.

The IRS Is a Great Ally

Several years ago I appeared as a guest on the television show *Issues,* which originated in Washington, D.C. The theme of the program was philanthropy. The other two guests were the commissioner of the Internal Revenue Service (IRS) and the chairman for a group of major philanthropic foundations in America. The moderator of the show asked me the first question: "Why do people give big gifts to philanthropic institutions?" I replied, "You're asking the wrong person. You should ask the head of the IRS." We all laughed, but we knew this answer had a great element of truth in it. The moderator went on to ask me the next question: "Do you think it is fair for someone to get a big tax deduction and then be saluted for making a gift? Specifically should someone get their name placed on a building and at the same time enjoy the benefits of paying less taxes because of the gift?" Again I replied, "You're asking the wrong person. You should visit a university on commencement day when young people are receiving diplomas for their chosen careers. The name of the auditorium or even the school bears a donor's name who gave a big gift and received a big tax benefit. Ask that student if he is glad the donor gave and the school is there. Or go to a hospital that bears the name of a donor and talk to a family waiting in the surgery area. Ask if they are pleased that the hospital is there. Or go to a church where the young people are playing in a gymnasium named for a donor who got a tax deduction and ask those kids or their families if they are glad the gym is there."

This is our American system. Thank God our founders and successors recognized the need to link philanthropy with tax savings in such a way that the donor could receive tax credit, and the state would have no control over the institutions who received the gift. It has been a great help in motivating gifts to develop our religious, educational, cultural, social, community, and other nonprofit institutions. The church should recognize this motivation for gifting, treasure it, support its continuance, and understand the system in order to raise more funds for its mission.

We call this gifting aid a tax shelter. We should all know how it works. When you make a gift, up to the maximum allowance of your gross income, you may claim it as a deduction from your income in determining your income tax.

The law now provides that the donor may claim this deduction for the year it is contributed and, if desired, may spread it over the succeeding five years for tax benefit.

You may give from proceeds earned in capital gains such as stocks, bonds, or real estate and avoid paying taxes on the amount of these gifts. Remember, in order to avoid these capital gains taxes, you must transfer these equities to the church and not sell them first and then give the proceeds to the philanthropic institution.

You may give gifts of cash, equity, real estate, etc., to your charity through your will or trust and avoid having these dollars go through probate at the time of the settlement. (This saves money and time in settling an estate.) Gifts designated for a nonprofit charity in the estate settlement are not subject to certain estate taxes. This may be a significant tax motivation for estate holders.

It is important for the donor to receive competent legal counsel on the provisions of using charitable gifts as tax shelters. The laws and regulations frequently change. It is important to have up-to-date guidance in your planned-giving strategy.

Using the IRS as a giving ally is good business. Individuals as well as businesses and corporations utilize these opportunities. It is good stewardship!

An important point for the church to stress is that the IRS tax provision for charity is not just for large donors. For example, regular contributions, regardless of size, given at weekly worship services are subject to the same rulings. The donor may use the total amount given to the church during the year as contributions up to the allowable deduction. Their church or other charity should be registered as a not-for-profit organization in order that they may receive such gifts as tax-deductible donations.

Here are some important points to remember:

- Pledges are not tax deductible. The donor may deduct only money or gifts of substance.
- A gift of cash over a certain amount, unless accompanied by an acknowledgment of the gift, is generally not accepted as a contribution deduction. Most routine giving is done through bank checks. A record of those checks is helpful. However, the IRS now requires a statement of receipt from the charity for most gifts. Your church should provide you with this to support your claim in your tax report.

An excellent system of giving for regular contributions to the church is the envelope system.

- It verifies the amount of the donor's gift.
- It keeps the donor regular in giving, since most envelopes are used on a calendar-dated basis.
- It keeps the donor current in his or her giving.
- It makes the donor feel significant. It makes each donor feel he or she belongs to a larger body.
- It will increase the church's financial support.

Giving Motivated out of Needs

Another reason people give to the church is because they are motivated to meet needs. Something in each of us compels us to respond to needs. The more obvious the need and the more viable the solution, the greater the response will be from the donor. The church must constantly make the congregation aware of its honest needs and opportunities for mission.

The donor will often give to one project over another. The church should respect this and encourage the donor to give to whatever seems most compelling. We should "scratch where they itch." Appealing to the donor's interest and involvement is often the key in developing larger gifts. Many people will give modest gifts out of routine and loyalty. Sometimes the only way to increase their giving is to expose them to larger opportunities and have them think "outside the box." Sometimes it's wise to expose the donor to greater challenges than the local church's mission only.

I once served as the pastor for a very wealthy congregation. I preached about the importance of giving. Our church was growing, so the needs were obvious. As is so often the case, we had a member with considerable wealth who gave two dollars a week. He had done this for years; I'm sure he felt satisfied with this. The way we lifted his giving to the church was to expose him to a larger mission cause. I introduced him to a seminary. He became interested in that opportunity to train ministers. He gave. That gift was developed into a major named endowment. I exposed him to the Presbyterian Foundation. He hosted a meeting in his home for the national foundation's chairman and executive to share with neighbors and friends the story of this vast giving program. He established a major trust through the foundation for giving to many validated ministries. What happened to his giving to the local church? It increased many times, and he became a leading contributor to the parish church. Exposure to the larger needs did it.

Church leaders should not be overanxious about competition for donors' gifts. Many times these opportunities for giving to other causes will develop giving to the congregation's mission.

The local church must think big. Its mission must embrace not just local causes but the needs of the world beyond. The more the congregation can give away, the more money it will take in.

People Give Because Someone Asks Them to Give

Inviting people to contribute to a cause is often the key to making it happen. It's so simple. If you want people to give, just ask them. This is so obvious, but it is the most unused key in the entire fund-raising procedure. We don't ask for the following reasons:

- *We are afraid to ask.* The worst that can happen is that the donor prospect says no. In fact, the donor prospect usually starts off by saying, "Let me think about it." Now you have your foot in the door, and it would not have happened if you hadn't asked.
- *We're not sure the donor prospect will give.* That's not the problem of the person making the appeal. Granted, we should not be asking for large gifts if we have reason to believe that the resources are not there for the prospect to respond. That is poor taste. Generally we know our prospects so we should inform, cultivate, and then ask.
- *We think the timing is wrong to ask.* Of course some circumstances make it untimely to ask for a gift. Timing is beyond our control. Many gifts have been missed because the donor wasn't given an opportunity to give in time. Their circumstances changed the possibility of a gift, or it went to another cause. Unfortunately those of us who have been around fund-raising for any time have illustrations of the problem caused by a delay in asking.
- *We are not sure of our cause.* Seek help and get information. Once you are satisfied and have a prospect that is ready to be solicited, you should ask for the commitment.

25

- *We are lazy.* Sometimes fund-raisers are lazy. Persistence is also very important. We usually don't get a commitment, especially a larger commitment, the first time we ask. There is great value in just "hanging in there." Remember the parable that Jesus told about the persistent widow?

> "There was in a certain city a judge who did not fear God nor regard man. Now there was a widow in that city; and she came to him, saying, 'Get justice for me from my adversary.' And he would not for a while; but afterward he said within himself, 'Though I do not fear God nor regard man, yet because this widow troubles me I will avenge her, lest by her continual coming she weary me.'"

> Luke 18:2–5

Fund-raising has much to learn from that parable. Just keep asking. Of course we don't recommend that you become obnoxious, but don't quit asking too soon.

A good rule of thumb is to keep asking until the donor makes a commitment or gives you a firm no. You must respect a no. You have done your part by informing, cultivating, and soliciting. You hope the donor prospect responds positively. If you receive a negative reply, move on to other candidates. However, time and circumstances may even turn a no into a yes later on.

Statistics vary on how many times you should ask, depending on the purpose of the campaign, the size of the gift being solicited, and the circumstances of the donor prospect. However, I know from experience that you often ask many times and in many ways. Remember the old adage "Rome wasn't built in a day"? Fund-raising campaigns take time, and leadership must be willing to devote time to accomplish the goal.

26

Remember, when you are soliciting, your focus is not on yourself but on the donor prospect. People are flattered to be asked to give. They may never know about your cause unless you inform them and ask them to give. People want to be identified with a cause. Someone must ask them to participate. That solicitor is the instrument. God is the source of the supply and the only one the donor prospect must answer to.

Without question, the key to giving is often simply being asked to give. So keep on asking. It will produce results.

People Give Because of the Rewards in Giving

- They give because it feels good.
- They give because they are spiritually blessed.
- They give because giving awards them recognition.
- They give because they become part of the solution.
- They give because it fine-tunes their relationship with others.
- They give because they receive some tangible gift in return for their giving. Donors treasure such gifts because they know they received them in return for their giving.
- People give because their cause is advanced through their gifts.

The well-ordered fund-raising plan takes into account all the reasons that people give and designs its appeal to touch every reason for giving and tailor the approach to where it will produce the greatest results.

~ 2 ~

WHY DO PEOPLE GIVE TO THE CHURCH?

Most reliable philanthropic sources indicate that Americans give away about $150 billion annually to charitable causes. That figure has grown enormously over the years. More Americans give every year, and people have more money to give away. Of the total dollars contributed to all nonprofit institutions in America, donations from individuals account for nearly 80 percent. The balance comes from foundations, corporations, and bequests. Religious organizations receive around 50 percent of all gifts, and the balance goes to education, human services, health, arts, culture, the humanities, social services, community projects, and various other nonprofits.

Of all the money given to religious causes, over two-thirds goes to Christian churches. Nearly all of that comes from individuals. These gifts range from very small contributions to major philanthropic donations. Statistics show that the individuals who regularly give the most money are:

- regular attenders at worship services
- active members of the congregation
- donors involved in congregational programs
- volunteers who give time and talent
- church leaders and officers

In addition, tithers are the highest per capita donors, yet only about 3–5 percent of the individuals who contribute to nonprofit organizations give 10 percent or more to religious causes. Also, people with a personal relationship with Christ have the most consistent and increased giving performance.

The following statistics give us reason for concern and challenge:

- Giving to church causes is generally declining. This is not true with some groups. Some of the philanthropic dollars are now going to causes that churches formerly sponsored.
- Parachurch ministries are making direct appeals to traditional congregations and getting strong dollar support.
- Nonchurch charitable organizations in many instances are doing a better job of soliciting and getting gifts than church institutions. For example, many colleges, universities, and other educational institutions, along with health, social services, and cultural groups, have full-time development staffs creating philanthropic gifts. Very few churches of any size have such a staff or ministers of stewardship.

- Budget crunches and the need for other professional staff account for this lack of hiring professionals whose major responsibility is to generate more income for the church.
- A staff person with development responsibilities will usually pay for his or her services many times through new income generated. However, many churches cannot consider filling this position professionally for practical reasons. However, I have consulted with some churches with members in their congregation who didn't need large salaries and had excellent service to offer. These people are attractive candidates for development services, especially if they have had people-oriented positions and know how to motivate others. These people are frequently successful development officers. However recruited, having a person in this critical position should be a "must" for many growing congregations.

Why do most people who give select the church as their favorite charity to support? They do so because the church plays such a major role in their lives. For many who give regularly and generously, the church has touched them as no other institution has.

- Their families may have been in the church when they were born.
- They were baptized or dedicated to the Lord in early childhood at the church.
- They attended Sunday school as children and learned the teaching of their religious faith and the spiritual reasons for their moral and ethical system.
- They were a part of the youth group, with its various character-development programs, where they met lifelong friends and spiritual mates.

- They have affirmed Christ as personal Savior and Lord of their lives through the church's life-changing programs.
- They may have had their faith confirmed in preparation for membership in the church.
- They may have been motivated for their life vocations through preparation courses in the church.
- They may have been influenced in selecting their educational goals and selecting schools for higher education through their church guidance program.
- They may have found their life companions in the fellowship of the church.
- They may have stood before the altar of the church and exchanged their marriage vows.
- They may have stood together as parents in the church and presented their children for baptism or dedication to the Lord.
- They may have joined family and friends in the church to memorialize a loved one who had passed on to be with the Lord.
- They may have volunteered countless hours to the outreach of the church.
- They may have formed their major social bonds in the fellowship experience in the church.
- They may have used their gifts and leadership skills to give direction and purpose to the church.
- The church may be like a golden thread that has run through the very fabric of their lives.

Naturally, anything that has been that important in shaping a person's life would receive that person's support.

Others may not have grown up in church. Yet perhaps in a time of crisis, the church created an atmosphere for a central life-changing experience. Through participation in worship, fellowship, educational programs, and counsel, things suddenly come together. They know that their church relationship is primarily responsible. Naturally they want to support the institution that has made a difference in their lives.

People support the church because the church has supported them. A few years ago, there was a clever saying, WIFM, which simply meant "What's in it for me?" This often became the fund-raiser's "pitch" in appealing for donor support. WIFM is not all there is to church support appeal, but it is a large contributing factor in generating donor support. All data measurements indicate that the greater the involvement in an institution, the more the constituents will support it with their money.

When we examine all the church does in our lives, we realize these great things don't just happen. The church is just like our families, our businesses, our communities, and our government. They all take money to survive and grow. It costs money to build the buildings, pay the utilities, and provide capable church workers. This money must come from the members and friends of the church. While, ultimately, all resources come from the Lord, the day-to-day resources needed for growth come directly through the people who use the church services.

In America the state does not support the church; the people do. The state offers tax incentives for giving that may enlarge the giving ability of donors, but the church money package is not a part of local, state, or federal government.

People give to the church to keep it going. Most other institutions in society seek support for the same reason. The church's support depends, in part, on how well it serves the people and how well the people are informed of its services. In order for a church to raise adequate funds, its worship services and programs need to attract people to its facilities. It must be concerned and skillful in discipling the attendees in their Christian faith. Churches must be credible in handling the money they receive and diligent in keeping donors informed.

People give to the church more than to any other cause. They give to the church because of what the church gives to them. If the church practices high integrity and good management, people will continue to support its projects.

Driven by Stewardship

Financial support for churches involves more than wise fund-raising principles. People give to the church out of a desire to be good stewards. Simply stated, stewardship means that God is the owner and we are managers of what he has allowed us to possess. This concept lifts our giving to the highest level. We give because we have no other alternative, if we are truly motivated to manage our sacred trust. We are stewards. All that we are comes from God. The world belongs to God. We belong to God. Stewardship says that we are holding something in trust for someone else. We are holding God's kingdom and its outreach in a trust capacity. This demands our constant attention and our faithful devotion. We are accountable.

Stewardship includes how we handle our money. But it is far more than that. Christian stewardship means how we manage our lives. It includes the wise use of our time, our talents, and our possessions. Stewardship becomes the grand design for living.

Stewardship lifts the congregation's fund-raising needs and appeal to a spiritual level, which will not only raise more money but enrich the donors in their spiritual growth.

Fund-raising says, "We need to raise money for our causes."

Stewardship says, "Serve God and be faithful in your generosity."

Fund-raising says, "How many dollars did we raise?"

Stewardship says, "How many congregants grew in grace?"

Fund-raising says, "Give and feel good."

Stewardship says, "Give because God says it is good."

Fund-raising says, "The successful response of the donors will make it happen."

Stewardship says, "God makes it happen through his stewards."

Stewardship is not just an ecclesiastical term for a way to get more money. It should become the constant message of the church in order to enlarge the mission of the church and enrich the lives of each contributor.

The core truths of Jesus' message are found in his parables. Eighteen of his parables deal with the stewardship of our material possessions.

One of these parables stresses the need for us to give according to our own capacity. It is called "the parable of the talents" and recorded in Matthew 25:14–30.

"For the kingdom of heaven is like a man traveling to a far country, who called his own servants and delivered his goods to them. And to one he gave five talents, to another two, and to another one, to each according to his own ability; and immediately he went on a journey. Then he who had received the five talents went and traded with them, and made another five talents. And likewise he who had received two gained two more also. But he who had received one went and dug in the ground, and hid his lord's money. After a long time the lord of those servants came and settled accounts with them.

"So he who had received five talents came and brought five other talents, saying, 'Lord, you delivered to me five talents; look, I have gained five more talents besides them.' His lord said to him, 'Well done, good and faithful servant; you were faithful over a few things, I will make you ruler over many things. Enter into the joy of your lord.' He also who had received two talents came and said, 'Lord, you delivered to me two talents; look, I have gained two more talents besides them.' His lord said to him, 'Well done, good and faithful servant; you have been faithful over a few things, I will make you ruler over many things. Enter into the joy of your lord.'

"Then he who had received the one talent came and said, 'Lord, I knew you to be a hard man, reaping where you have not sown, and gathering where you have not scattered seed. And I was afraid, and went and hid your talent in the ground. Look, there you have what is yours.'

"But his lord answered and said to him, 'You wicked and lazy servant, you knew that I reap where I have not sown, and gather where I have not scattered seed. So you ought to have deposited my money with the bankers, and at my coming I would have received back my own with interest. So take the talent from him, and give it to him who has ten talents.

"'For to everyone who has, more will be given, and he will have abundance; but from him who does not have, even what he has will be taken away. And cast the unprofitable servant into the outer darkness. There will weeping and gnashing of teeth.'"

This is a very provocative lesson. It provides a template for managing our lives. It says that Christian growth is not measured by our gifts alone but by the individual integrity that we bring to our own capacities. This parable says, "Use it or lose it." Our fidelity will be rewarded; our neglect will be condemned. Stewardship is the profile of how we handle our capacities. What are we doing with what we have been given? Whatever our gifts may be, we should treasure them, cultivate them, and increase them. This diagram for getting the most out of life includes "the giving of the increase of our substance." This serving and high calling moves our appeal for funds from sheer fund-raising efforts to the essence of discipleship. This parable should become the rubric of the church's development program.

Another parable that Jesus told gives us the priority for ordering our lives toward victorious living. Luke 12:16–21 records this message:

> Then He spoke a parable to them, saying: "The ground of a certain rich man yielded plentifully. And he thought within himself, saying, 'What shall I do, since I have no room to store my crops?' So he said, 'I will do this: I will pull down my barns and build greater, and there I will store all my crops and my goods. And I will say to my soul, "Soul, you have many goods laid up for many years; take your ease; eat, drink, and be merry!"' But God said to him, 'Fool! This night your soul will be required of you; then whose will those things be which you have provided?'
>
> "So is he who lays up treasure for himself, and is not rich toward God."

This story is often called "the parable of the rich fool." The end result of the rich man's life purpose gave him the title "fool." From all other perspectives, he seemed successful.

- He appeared to have succeeded in his vocation. He was wealthy.
- He seemed to have acquired his wealth honestly.
- He was thrifty. He saved his money for an emergency.
- He apparently was a good spender. He was planning to provide employment for others.
- He wasn't a grasping miser. He planned to retire and let others take his position.
- There's no reason to believe he wasn't a moral and ethical person.

Where did he go wrong? His value system was founded on material things instead of eternal things.

- He apparently had no spiritual values to lift his business acumen.
- He thought he could live forever on the temporary provisions of corn and oats.
- He thought he owned the world.
- He completely disregarded God—the source of all he had.
- His stewardship was self-centered.
- He thought of nothing beyond the temporal and material.

Nothing is wrong with working hard and acquiring. Money is not the problem. It's how we use it that determines our merit. Money is eternally empty in itself, but money linked to God may work wonders. Building bigger barns just to have bigger barns is empty. Using the barn-building money to enrich the lives of others makes the difference in life's success or failure, according to Jesus.

These two parables of Jesus along with the other teachings in the Bible on this important subject of stewardship must be the starting point in creating a fundraising system for the truly successful church.

The Terrific Tenet of Tithing

The stewardship equation begins with God. We have each been trusted with a portion of God's wealth with which to manage our own lives and help the lives of others. Proportionate giving is the systematic method of accomplishing this. We put God at the top of our giving objectives. We set aside a proportionate amount to build God's kingdom. The Bible states clearly that this proportional gift standard starts with 10 percent given to God for his kingdom's work. This is the principle of *tithing.*

This fund-raising standard of giving away 10 percent has been a key instrument of the church from its beginning. In nearly a lifetime's career in raising funds, I have worked for clients in the fields of education, health, community and social services, culture and the arts, and religion. Of all these causes, the church is the only one where tithing has been a natural and focused guide. It is biblical and historically practiced and emphasized. Many times I have said, in seminars for church leaders, "If there is only one thing I can leave with you as counsel that is sure to succeed in raising funds for your church, it is the principle of tithing. Promote it, teach it, preach it, practice it." This is the most certain way to achieve financial success in the church.

I've seen this emphasis on tithing turn churches around. One church that had been around since 1625 and had difficulty meeting its financial demands decided to make tithing central in its congregational appeal. Giving increased enormously and the church moved from want to outreach.

My first church after seminary was a Presbyterian church in Oregon. Like many moderate-sized congregations, it was struggling to pay its bills and support missions. I had only been the pastor for a short time when I attended my first board meeting. I was the youngest member present. A disturbing financial report was given. The problem was clear: the income from the congregation was not sufficient to meet the church's financial demands. Should we cut the budget? There wasn't much to cut. Could we raise money? From whom? So I made a bold suggestion. I proposed that we start a tithing club and that we all become charter members. I reminded the other members that they all knew my income. They had approved the terms of my call as pastor. I had no other source of income. I dramatically said that I would be the first member of the tithing club and figuratively threw my 10 percent on the table. My idea "went over like a lead balloon." No one had much to say. It became very quiet. We soon adjourned. The tithing club had one member: *me.*

When the meeting was over, I was busy picking up some meeting materials and noticed the clerk of the session was just hanging around. Finally Loren said to me, "I'm sorry I didn't speak up during your tithing club appeal. I'm retired and living on a modest railroad pension. Ten percent of my income isn't very much, but I believe in the tithing principle." We now had two members in the newly organized tithing club. Loren and I met every Saturday night in my office to pray together for the Sunday services and our church's needs. We invited the other elders to join us. At first none came. As time went on, our Saturday night meeting increased and our tithing club grew. We did not make a big thing out of it. We didn't create a "club" concept where some felt superior and others felt inferior. We have no right to put a guilt trip on the congregation. We just quietly talked about tithing and its means to Christian growth. The tithing principle seemed to grow by osmosis.

A few years later, the congregation membership had increased by over 100 percent. We were financially solvent and had a strong benevolence budget. Denominational leaders told us that our church was leading its division of churches in per capita giving. The only reason we could give was that God gave the increase. The tithing principle was the key human element.

Today that church is a very strong congregation. A few years before I arrived, the Presbytery had met on the site of the church to dissolve the pitifully small congregation and close the church. Only one active member truly cared. He begged the Presbytery not to close it yet. He asked if he could keep the keys of the church. Every Sunday he opened the doors. He was the only one there. He finally engaged a college student who was planning to go on to seminary to become the minister. This student could sing and talk. Gradually others began to attend services. The rest of the story is history. When the good retired doctor said, "Give me the keys," that kept the church from closing.

A few years later, the tithing club made a big difference. The principle of tithing is the key factor in developing funds to operate and build a church.

Many years later, I was consulting with a large congregation whose membership numbered in the thousands. But just as in my first congregation, the need for more income was critical. I shared the tithing principle advice and mentioned our quiet little tithing club from years earlier. Those attending the meeting thought it was a great idea. They grabbed the club concept and ran with it with gusto. Too much gusto! Almost immediately it became a snooty clique. Those who tithed were "in";

those who did not were "out." Such an approach is wrong and harmful to a congregation.

Questions about Tithing

A harsh legal approach to the tithing principle is not a fitting spirit. Tithing is a personal response to God's call for stewardship. Each person should respond to that call with sincere devotion.

Of course, thoughtful guidance may be helpful, as it is with any spiritual principle. I'll give you my thoughts on the frequently asked questions. However, I will not put them out as mandates or axioms but simply my responses to questions I frequently have been asked.

Should the tithe be calculated on the before-income tax figure or after? Thoughts vary on this. Jesus seems to say "before." The Pharisees were questioning him on the subject of paying taxes. He said:

> "Show me the tax money." And they brought Him a denarius.
> And He said to them, "Whose image and inscription is this?"
> They said to Him, "Caesar's." And He said to them, "Render therefore to Caesar the things that are Caesar's, and to God the things that are God's."
>
> Matthew 21:19–21

You may choose to base your tithe differently. But however you calculate it, I encourage you to start practicing the tithing principle of proportionate giving.

Should the tithe include other philanthropic causes? Many will point out that much of what is now accomplished by these other causes, such as health, education, and social organizations, was formerly performed by the church. They might suggest that these causes therefore may be considered our tithe. I agree with the logic of that argument; others may disagree. I would encourage a proportional amount of the tithe go to the church in relation to its need and the donor's involvement with it.

Should the "storehouse" be limited to the local congregation? The Bible says, "Bring all the tithes into the storehouse" (Mal. 3:10a). In years past, the local mission of the congregation represented the major amount of ministry. Churches associated with denominations, as most were, gave their "benevolence" dollars for others through their church boards and agencies. Today's ministry is far more diversified. Many local congregations are meeting their mission challenge with parachurch ministries and other mission causes. Many large donors now give major funds to other causes.

While the trend is toward a larger and more diverse ministry outreach, we must encourage the local congregation to meet the needs of the local mission and to maintain the designated mission they have funded. At the same time, we must encourage them to think outside the box and to make the mission dollars reach as far as possible.

The tithing principle is the single most important button to push for raising the most dollars within a congregation. However, the dollar amount that the tithing principle generates is small in comparison to what it does for the tither. Tithing will give a direction to one's total financial package that may turn the tide from failure to success.

Several years ago, the Gallup organization did a survey on tithing in America. They asked people three questions:

- Do you tithe (10 percent)?
- Do you know anyone who tithes (10 percent)?
- Do the tithers you know have financial problems?

The answers were revealing:

- 22 percent of the survey people did tithe
- 46 percent knew people who did tithe
- 87 percent of people who tithed did not have financial problems

The purpose for tithing is not to make money. It is not an "ecclesiastical slot machine." But it works out that the tither is better off. Tithing develops the core of God's money management. It develops budget structure for the donor and family. Tithing requires discipline. Discipline establishes order. Order creates success. Tithing puts God first. The Scriptures say:

> Honor the LORD with your possessions,
> And with the firstfruits of all your increase;
> So your barns will be filled with plenty,
> And your vats will overflow with new wine.
>
> Proverbs 3:9–10

Tithing takes the guesswork out of giving. You establish a tithing fund and you have money available when the call is made.

Tithing will make you a stronger Christian. Whatever gets in your head gets you. Jesus said, "For where your treasure is, there your heart will be also" (Matt. 6:21).

Tithing has a definite reward for the tither. The Bible says:

> "Bring all the tithes into the storehouse,
> That there may be food in My house,

44

And try Me now in this,"
Says the LORD of hosts,
"If I will not open for you the windows of heaven
And pour out for you such blessing
That there will not be room enough to receive it."

Malachi 3:10

What an amazing promise! And it works! I've never met a retired tither! People who truly practice it over a reasonable period of time would never consider not tithing. The dollar amounts may vary, as their circumstances or seasons of life may vary, but the principle of giving God the first 10 percent is nonnegotiable.

I watched my own mother live on a very limited retirement income in her later years. But she always tithed to the Lord's work. She got the "biggest bang for her buck" of the remaining 90 percent. I've talked to many tithers who will confirm this principle. "I'll never quit tithing; I can't afford to."

Tithing should be the core message of the church in designing its money appeal programs:

- Preach it. Teach it. Get the people to give it a fair test.
- Getting started is hard. It takes faith. One reason is because so many people have nothing left after paying their bills. Nearly 30 percent of our population say they nearly always have money problems. How can you start tithing if you have nothing to tithe with? It's a matter of distributing.
- Start with a commitment to God and yourself that you will become a tither.
- Begin with a percentage figure you can live with after you make achievable spending allocations.

- Make the decision and get started. The results will amaze you.
- Give yourself a one-year trial program.

Proportional giving develops Christian loyalty. Church budgets, programs, mission needs, and church development machinery are all secondary. The primary reason for a Christian's proportional giving is *internal*. It's the mark of stewardship, and stewardship is a measure of our growth in Christian grace. Settling this real reason for giving to the church will make our search for outlets for resources most effective.

These outlets are generally the result of needs. The church must keep the people aware of the needs. These needs must be viable and presented in a winsome form to the donors. If the church has done an effective job of creating the principles of stewardship as a normal part of congregational life, and if the stewardship program is driven by the tenets of tithing, the church will be sure of dollars to satisfy its mission.

<svg>decorative flourish</svg>

3

THE THEOLOGY
OF GIVING

In lecturing to pastors and other church leaders on the subject of fund-raising, I have often opened my remarks with the question "How many of you find it difficult to preach or talk with your congregation about money?" Each time, many will say yes or raise their hands.

Often their thoughts are on "things of the Spirit" as they should be. The subject of fund-raising may have low priority. Generally speaking, colleges and seminaries prepare prospective ministers to do their jobs effectively and fulfill their calling. Courses do not focus on the subject of money. Few even include it in their curriculum, although, of necessity, more institutions are beginning to offer the practical subjects of how to make a church work.

When I was in seminary, my interests were biblical languages, theology, church history, and the Bible. Each

47

of these subjects is important and exciting but does not adequately prepare church leaders for "running the store." I started out as a parish pastor and planned to be only that for the rest of my life. That was my calling, a marvelous and honorable calling. However, I hadn't been in the role of shepherding a congregation long before I discovered it took money to feed the sheep. Rather than passing this function along to the laypeople, I became convinced that the subject of money is at the heart of life ministry. An awesome subject, it speaks to much of what life is about.

At our house we talk about money as much as any other subject. You do the same. Oh, we don't just sit around and say, "Now let's talk about money." But the subject is everywhere. My wife says, "I'm going to the store to get some things." Before she gets out of the store she pays with money. I go to the mailbox. Inside are bills requesting money for payment. Advertisements make glittering appeals to purchase something for money. Appeals from our church and from charities request money to keep their programs going. Banks and other financial institutions send out statements informing us of the status of our money. On and on it goes. Money constantly screams for our attention.

Any subject that is so interwoven in the fabric of our lives cannot be treated casually or put aside. Money is a critical subject for the church. Not only is money necessary to pay the bills of the church, but the subject of money is important to discipling the congregation.

The Bible speaks frequently about material possessions and how we handle them, as often as nearly any other subject. Someone has calculated that prayer is mentioned about five hundred times in the Bible, faith is mentioned more than five hundred times, and how we handle our resources is mentioned over a thousand times.

48

The subject of fund-raising is bound up in what people believe about giving. Giving makes fund-raising happen, and giving has enormous spiritual overtones.

In fact, giving is the core of our Christian theological system. "We live to give and we give to live." Here is the logic of this theology.

God is a giving creature. The psalmist said, "The earth is the LORD's, and all its fullness" (Ps. 24:1). He made it. He owns it. He chose to share it. Genesis is the account of God spinning out his energy and creating the heavens, the earth, light, waters, firmament, grass, herbs, trees, fruits, birds, fish, animals. When God saw all that he had made, he "saw that it was good" (Gen. 1:25). Creation was the earliest account of the dynamic of giving. It exhibited the nature of God.

Humans are designed to be giving creatures. "Then God said, 'Let Us make man in Our image, according to Our likeness; let them have dominion over the fish of the sea, over the birds of the air, and over the cattle, over all the earth and over every creeping thing that creeps on the earth.' So God created man in His own image; in the image of God He created him; male and female He created them" (Gen. 1:26–27). That's who we are—the created image of God. So who is God? The Bible defines God this way: "God is love" (1 John 4:8). When you think of the word *love*, the highest and most definitive word to explain this quality in action is the word *giving*. That is who God is—a giving God. In this context *love* is a noun and *giving* is an active participle. That means that God has always been giving; he is giving now and he will continue giving forever. As Christians we believe we see God personified on earth in the person of Jesus Christ. The Bible confirms this eternal character when it proclaims that "Jesus Christ is the same yesterday, today, and forever" (Heb. 13:8). Jesus Christ shows us God's image. We are made in God's image, and God came to earth in the person of Jesus Christ to exhibit God's essence.

Humanity is at its best when it is giving, because that is the essence of who God is. Humanity is at its worst when it is not giving. In essence that may be at the root of the word *sin*. Theologians have defined sin as "missing the mark." If the target, the "mark," is to reflect God's image, which is giving, we really miss the target when we are selfish, mean, petty, and greedy.

Why are we not always giving? How could we miss the mark of giving? Philosophers would say that for giving to be real there must be an opportunity to not give. The choice makes giving meaningful. The Bible tells the story, and history corroborates it, that mankind makes selfish choices. The story of Adam and Eve in the Book of Genesis personifies this part of our nature. Adam and Eve's selfishness changed everything. They were no longer motivated to give but to take and hide. The rest of the Bible is the story of this struggle and how mankind kept "missing the mark." God kept giving and giving and finally "gave His only begotten Son, that whoever believes in Him should not perish but have everlasting life" (John 3:16). God's giving nature made it possible to restore our relationship with him. Through grace, mankind can "hit the mark." That redemptive act of God in Christ not only furnished us with a living example of his giving nature but made it possible for humanity to repent and turn about-face. By grace, this has all happened. Not of our own doing; it is the "gift of God."

Through faith we accept this gift and take on the design that God intended us to have in the first place. We have the opportunity to reflect God's image and real purpose for living. As this redeemed new creature in Christ, we live to give and we give to live. Paul said it this way: "If anyone is in Christ, he is a new creation; old things have passed away; behold, all things have become new" (2 Cor. 5:17). In other words, we are no longer living just for self but for others. The miserly, grasping, selfish nature has become giving, sharing, and radiant.

While preaching in Athens, Paul talked about the true God "who gives to all life, breath, and all things." He went on to say, "He has made from one blood every nation of men to dwell on all the face of the earth, . . . so that they should seek the Lord, in the hope that they might grope for Him and find Him, though He is not far from each one of us; for in Him we live and move and have our being" (Acts 17:25–28).

Then Paul brought together all these thoughts on the subject when he wrote, "For to me, to live is Christ" (Phil. 1:21).

Look at the sequence of these verses:

- "For in Adam all die, even so in Christ all shall be made alive" (1 Cor. 15:22). After Christ, mankind had a second chance to become a fully giving creature again.
- "In faith count yourself dead to selfishness and alive to giving through Jesus Christ" (Rom. 6:11).

This renewed image of God, this giving creator, evidences itself in all of life. Paul speaks about the new life in Christ, which shows itself in what he calls the fruit of the Spirit: "love, joy, peace, longsuffering, kindness, goodness, faithfulness, gentleness. . . . If we live in the Spirit, let us also walk in the Spirit" (Gal. 5:22–25).

Each of these fruits is activated by a giving spirit. As you reflect on the "fruit of the Spirit" mentioned by Paul, you will see that the attitude and activity to make it happen is "giving."

Think what will happen when giving becomes the driving force for our behaviors. This is what can happen to the new creature in Christ.

Transfer that thought to the areas where we all live:

Family. When the husband and wife are each driven to give to each other, they have established the "true bonds of matrimony." It will make the difference in success or failure of this blessed union. If the relationship is bound by giving, there can be no place for infidelity, neglect, or violence. The new life in Christ is a catalyst for this mutual grace of giving. When parents see their children as a prime focus for their giving, they will develop a bond and kindness that becomes enduring. Giving binds siblings, cousins, grandparents, grandchildren, and every family relationship.

Friends. A friend is defined as "a person whom one knows well and is fond of." Friends are very important in this life. Some people we know will be our friends for an entire lifetime. The action that sustains and develops friendship is the act of giving. Friends are people who give you their support, their trust, their confidence, and their help. You can always count on them to be giving when you need it the most. You know that they are willing and responsive to your giving. If these qualities are lacking on either side of the relationship, a true friendship doesn't exist. We judge and keep our friends on the basis of this positive expression of giving.

Workplace. We see the importance of giving as the key to harmony in the workplace. Whatever the trade, profession, vocation, or position, the person motivated to give to his or her associates, the company, and the customers will be the happiest. Their business will succeed better. They will work their way up the corporate ladder. They will be happier on the job if they are truly giving people.

Employers who are motivated by the same principles of giving will develop a greater loyalty and output from among their employees. Companies have been turned around from loss to gain by giving more to their employees. No company or corporation can truly succeed without this benchmark of giving, quid pro quo. Perhaps we could even restate the Golden Rule: "Give to others, as you would have others give to you." This little changing of the words "do" to "give" may bring the rule into clear focus. We give.

How our world would be changed if we replaced taking with giving. I've never heard of a war that started because both sides wanted to give to each other. History, instead, is full of stories of people who took from others, and hostilities resulted.

This principle of giving rather than taking and keeping may be at the root of our faith system. It is certainly consistent with who God is and is amply verified in Scripture.

We started this chapter by addressing the subject of money. It is sometimes a difficult subject for church leaders. They defend their position by saying the subject isn't spiritual enough. I'm suggesting that it may be a major tenet of our whole theology. Jesus was adamant on this point. Mark records the story this way:

> Now as He was going out on the road, one came running, knelt before Him, and asked Him, "Good Teacher, what shall I do that I may inherit eternal life?"
>
> So Jesus said to him, ". . . You know the commandments: 'Do not commit adultery,' 'Do not murder,' 'Do not steal,' 'Do not bear false witness,' 'Do not defraud,' 'Honor your father and your mother.'"
>
> And he answered and said to Him, "Teacher, all these things I have kept from my youth."

> Then Jesus, looking at him, loved him, and said to him, "One thing you lack: Go your way, sell whatever you have and give to the poor, and you will have treasure in heaven; and come, take up the cross, and follow Me."
>
> Mark 10:17–21

The emphasis Jesus placed on giving in this story certainly qualifies the subject as a major benchmark in determining priorities for a truly Christian system of theology.

In his letter to the church of Corinth, Paul emphasized the things that really mattered in determining the qualities for a Christian life. He concluded with this order: "Now abide faith, hope, love, these three; but the greatest of these is love" (1 Cor. 13:13). Henry Drummond wrote a book on 1 Corinthians 13 and called it *The Greatest Thing in the World*.

How do you recognize love? Love becomes visible in the act of giving. Giving is not just sharing our material possessions. It also means giving our time, talents, good thoughts, counsel, prayers, sympathy, protection, and anything we can share to enrich the lives of others. It certainly includes as a top priority the giving and sharing of our material possessions. Giving money is a true evidence of God's grace in our lives.

Giving is not a subject we should confine to a little talk once a year during "stewardship season." It is a subject that we should put before the people constantly. You can empower your church with the theology of giving. Church leaders must give it their attention. Not only will it pay the bills and build the church, but it will also create fertile soil for development and growth in Christian grace of the congregation.

4

THE ANATOMY
OF A GIFT

You can take the guesswork out of generating gifts if you use tested principles. I call this structure the *anatomy of a gift*. This chapter will be a detailed analysis of the major points and the timing for successful fund-raising. These principles apply whether the appeal is for operating expenses, capital needs, endowment funds, or even, to some extent, for raising deferred or estate gifts.

The template and timing for most fund-raising appeals will generally follow this order:

- needs package
- relevance

- information
- cultivation
- involvement
- solicitation and follow-up
- commitment
- acknowledgment
- collection procedures

You should use these nine points in order in every fund-raising effort you undertake.

Needs Package - 91,000

Before you begin asking for funds, you must have a bona fide need for the use of the funds. You may need to support the annual operating budget. You may need to purchase property. You may need to repair, improve, or exchange the buildings on the property. You may need to construct new buildings on the existing or additional properties. You may need to establish endowment funds to create a future "stream of income" for maintaining the buildings and property or extending the programs of the church. You may need future estate dollars for any of the needs mentioned above. In every case, the "needs package" must be carefully and prayerfully developed, containing the facts and figures to support your request for funds. You should present these needs in the most attractive package possible so that the needs will "cry out" to prospective donors, motivating them to give. After developing a bona fide needs package, your next step is to find donors who will underwrite the needs. This takes us to the second step in the anatomy of a gift.

56

Relevance

A gift begins with relevance. Prospective donors must generally have some relationship to the cause for which the appeal is being made. You can't simply stand on a street corner and generate philanthropic dollars; you must go where the relationships are. Creating a prospect list for donors is the next phase after determining the needs package.

Potential Donors

Natural sources of relevance will be found primarily through the following:

Church members. People give more to the church if they are official members or active participants. Of course, this is not the primary reason for taking people into membership. The purpose for receiving people into the church is to disciple believers. However, all studies indicate that a major by-product of church membership is greater financial support. All members should be considered as prospects for a congregational appeal. The only criterion is that they participate to the best of their ability.

Families of church members. Families of church members are often relevant as prospects for a fund-raising appeal. This is especially true in raising capital funds for a building program. Sometimes, parents of children who are church members are asked to give. Sometimes, children of parents who are members are asked to give. The same may be true of brothers, sisters, and other relatives. A family of a church member may combine gifts in memory or honor of a family member or name. This area of family relevance should be carefully studied and not overlooked.

Friends of church members. Sometimes friends and business or professional associates are bona fide prospects, even though they do not belong to or attend the church making the appeal. This is especially true where the purpose of the appeal may be of interest to the friend or associate. I have seen church members who were part of a business community that made philanthropic gifts request and receive gifts from their associates. Often this is a quid pro quo arrangement within the business organization. Such gifts are worth exploring, especially for capital needs. If the church member feels comfortable in guiding the solicitation, such a relationship can be a source for a significant gift. The relevance is in the relationship. Occasionally, the by-product from such a gift is that the friends or business associates will visit the church where they made an investment and become active in the church themselves. The gift opened the door!

Church worship attendees. People will sometimes attend worship and other special services with some regularity but not choose to become members. They are financially capable of supporting the gift appeal. These attendees often meet the criteria of relevance and should be considered as prospects.

Participants in church-related activities. Many churches sponsor and/or provide space for self-enrichment programs. Sometimes the people attending these programs have no other relationship with the church. I have seen major gifts developed from people in such auxiliary groups. The program involvement creates the relevance. If these people are highly involved in another church, good taste requires that care be taken to avoid aggressive solicitation. Some groups may simply be renting the facilities from the church in order to have space to meet. This group would usually not be relevant prospects for a church fund-raising cause. However, some of the people attending these programs may have some interest in your church's needs. This is particularly true of capital fund-raising.

Community. Prospects can also be found within the community where the church is located, people who are not members and might not participate in any of the church's activities. If the purpose of the fund-raising appeal has value for the citizens of the community, then an appeal may be effective. I have seen large gifts developed from these people where the use of the money provided space or programs for community enrichment. Again, the church should recognize that some people in the community already give to their own churches. It is important that the church be involved in community enrichment if it seeks to solicit funds from the community. Wherever possible, it is wise for the pastoral staff to be active in community activities such as schools, social programs, service clubs, and inter-congregational causes.

Denominational affiliation. Often a church will belong to a denomination, association, or network of churches where relevance for fund-raising will exist. These relationships are often the source for significant funding. The capital for many new congregations will come from these sources. Program enrichment will also have appeal to these related organizations. A group of churches that I have served as executive director has been a source of funds for causes within this network of churches. This network includes pastors from all denominations and traditions. Because of the relationships developed in this network, a relevance is established for successful appeal for funds. Every congregation should carefully consider an appeal to other organizations where their cause will have mutual interest.

Businesses and corporations. The key to corporate and business giving to churches is largely through the corporate officers and business leaders who are involved with the church making the appeal. Family businesses are often a source of funding where some members of the business organization have relevance with the church making the appeal. In times past, the business community performed its philanthropy primarily on a quid pro quo basis, making gifts largely to causes related to their businesses. I recall that when I directed fund-raising campaigns for colleges and universities we would aggressively solicit corporations whose products related to the degree programs of the school's graduates. These students were potential future employees of the businesses. If the campaigning school were an engineering school, we would pinpoint our solicitation to corporations who needed engineers. If the school were a business school, we would pinpoint the banking and business community. Today the direction of corporate solicitation has changed. Many corporations and businesses give to social, educational, and enrichment causes where no product relationships exist. However, churches generally are not considered for such gifts unless the purpose of the campaign includes social, educational, or self-enrichment programs. Many corporations have a "matching gift" policy where they will match the gift of an employee to a philanthropic appeal. Usually church appeals are not considered for a "matching gift" unless part of the fund-raising appeal may be separated for educational or social purposes. I have worked with churches where this has been done with success. Some relevance to the business and corporate world may be possible and should be explored.

Foundations. Some large national foundations may focus on giving to programs that are similar to those planned by your church. If you discover a foundation that has a stated purpose and/or history of giving similar to your needs, write and ask for a copy of their most recent annual report. Examine their giving records and the names of their board of directors and other officers. If you have a network that will lead you to a person in the foundation, follow up with that lead. If not, create a request to the foundation's grant personnel. Be sure that the request is not limited to your own parish program needs, as such requests usually do not fall within major foundations' grant provisions. Design your request with a larger appeal. Usually, smaller foundations, local foundations, and family foundations are the best sources for church-related appeals. While not a primary source of relevance, foundations may be worth serious exploration, remembering that foundations manage large amounts of money that must be given away.

These are the usual sources for gifts for a church appeal. Start with these prospective donors. Design your strategy for solicitation to these prospects and prioritize them generally in the order listed.

Getting the Attention of Other Potential Donors

Sometimes a church does not have significant names in the normal relevant sources in order to raise the funds needed. Here are some ways to get the attention of people outside your current constituency.

Newspapers

Newspapers may become a marvelous tool for developing relevance. Get acquainted with the religious editor of your local newspaper. Plant stories in the paper about upcoming events and significant people in the congregation.

Purchase ads in the local paper. Make certain that your ads say something to interest readers in attending your church. Make sure that the location of the church, time of service, and program participants are accurate. Make your ads attractive. Design them to stand out on the page. Develop special events such as music and drama, or celebrity and popular speakers to attract attendance. Place ads and stories in the newspaper to promote these events. I've always felt that there is a relationship between the ads you place in your newspaper and the stories the paper will run about your activities. Strategically timed and placed ads are usually well worth the time and money invested. To a lesser degree, ads in the yellow pages of your telephone directory also will attract people to your church, especially newcomers to the community. All of these printed advertisements can enlarge the relevance base of your church.

Radio and television

These media can be used in many ways to enlarge your relevance base. In whatever ways you use the media, make certain that your efforts are first class and attractive. The eyes and ears of the listening and viewing audience can move away from your message in an instant if it doesn't grab and hold them.

Spot TV ads have become a successful tool for developing relevance. These short media "bites" are generally personality driven. Two pastors I knew in Texas developed outstanding TV spot ads. In both cases, the messages are attractive because the pastors do not come across as stereotypical clergy but rather as people whom the viewers would like to know. The settings and content for the most effective spot ads generally are not "churchy." A focused message that speaks to the needs of the viewers works best. Due to time constraints, these ads must be fast and upbeat. These types of productions have proven successful in attracting new people to congregations. It is wise to get professional advice in designing the ads and competent direction in producing them. Consult a pastor who has done this successfully. Through your networking, seek out someone in the television ad world to give you professional advice and direction. Don't trust the making of these ads to someone inexperienced. Television spot ads do not allow for second chances. They should be designed to come off successfully the first time they run. With competent guidance, they can become an enormous instrument in generating new prospects for your congregation.

Radio. Many years ago I served as the organizing pastor of a church in Marin County, California. This church was the first of its denomination to come into this county, and few people who lived in the area at that time had belonged to this denomination in other locations. We had no church building or identification in the community, only the use of a small women's clubhouse, two hours per week, for our worship service. We rang doorbells and had small meetings in the homes of our base group members. Our growth was slow. At that time a new radio station opened in the community, the first station ever in that community. I went to the management and asked for a fifteen-minute radio slot for a talk and music program on Sunday afternoons. They were anxious to fill the time and I was anxious to get on the air, so I became the host for a program called *Words and Music.* I sang a song, gave a brief upbeat message, and told the people about our new church group. It was what they called then a "sustaining show"—the airtime was free. Everything in those days was live broadcasting. I showed up every Sunday afternoon and conducted my little radio show. To my delight and surprise, people listened to the program. The station allowed me to mention my new congregation and when and where we met together on Sunday. As a result of that simple show, listeners attended the church service and helped develop our congregation.

If you decide to use radio as a means for developing your church, focus on contacting a station that will reach your own community. Designing a national show is totally different. *Words and Music* never went beyond our community, which was never our intent. But it helped build our church. We bought some property and built a building. In 1997 that church celebrated its fiftieth anniversary. Today it is a thriving congregation, and one of the helpful start-up elements was that little radio show.

Years later I had the privilege of hosting a radio show called *Facing Life.* My regular colleague on that show was the pastor of a large church in Orange County, California. On each program we featured a dialogue on a subject of interest to the listeners. We used the recorded choral music from the church's first-rate choir for our musical feature, and we taped our verbal interview in the church. We purchased a simple but good-quality audio recorder and had a good sound engineer from the other pastor's congregation. Our production costs were minor. Our airtime was modest because we were on a station that largely was limited to reach the area where his church was located. On each program we identified the church, its location, and the service times. We encouraged people to "write in." A member of the staff called on these people. It worked. It brought people to the church that otherwise might not have attended.

You may want to use the radio media as a tool to enlarge your relevance base. If you should do this, keep the program format simple and attractive to the listeners. Seek out a station that reaches people within driving distance of your church. You don't need to spend much money on this. Design it for your own community, not as a national radio program. It worked for me and for others with whom I have worked. Use your connections with experienced sound people and your local radio station to get it started.

Television. You may use television as another means for enlarging your relevance base. Of course, this medium is much different because it includes visual elements as well as sound. If your purpose is to enlarge your church, design the program and coverage to reach the viewers in your general community. It may be a talk show featuring the pastor of the church or it may be a telecast of your Sunday worship services. Whatever your format, do it well. Make sure that the physical setting is pleasant, the speaker is attractive, the message is relevant, and the music is good. You will face a lot of competition for the viewers' attention but try this medium if you and your church have the talent and resources to carry it out.

Robert H. Schuller started his *Hour of Power* program many years ago not necessarily to become a worldwide television show but as a means for bringing more people to his church. The TV show was so successful that it has become the oldest and most widely viewed weekly religious show in history. It has all the right elements: a beautiful setting, an eloquent host, magnificent music, and a compelling guest personality interview. The *Hour of Power* television show stands out as an amazing far-reaching ministry that has helped millions. I had the privilege of working by Dr. Schuller's side for many years, frequently traveling with him. In airports, on the crowded city streets, in hotels, and at public gatherings, he was recognized. People wanted to meet him; the public treated him as a celebrity. When talking with him, they generally said something such as "Your ministry changed my life." Schuller has a worldwide impact on the spirituality of millions, which is the major impact of this television show. At the same time, *Hour of Power* has become a major instrument for developing his congregation and giving a broad base of relevance in generating funds. My primary role at the church was fund-raising. Many of the largest gifts came not from people involved in the local congregation but from viewers of the television show. I recall some who gave major gifts who had never been on the church campus. Their viewership created the relevance for soliciting the gift.

Television is a superb tool for ministry. If you are a pastor of a church and have the inclination to go on TV, carefully consider your goals, objectives, and costs. Several years ago I was encouraged to host a religious television show. A solid group of people urged me along. I was not operating from a congregational base with a church building. We had to rent a professional studio; create an attractive two-room set; and hire a professional director, camera crew, production people, and office staff to make it happen. Other than what the initial "encouragement group" contributed, our show depended upon weekly gifts from viewers. I was surprised at the support we received, but it became clear to me after months of telecasting that something was missing. We had no home base, no place to point the viewers to go. After trying it for a long period of time, we released our time slot to a large congregation that had a beautiful, big sanctuary, an outstanding preacher, and great music.

When they took our time slot, they had a location to encourage viewers to attend. Their program aired for several years and became a great factor in enlarging their congregation and building a relevance base. I share this story to point out that a calling to be a televangelist is a special one, and you must be committed to make it work. If you decide to try using TV to enlarge your congregation, use your church building for the setting, your congregation as the audience, and your regular church music, pulpit, and guests. Begin by seeking airtime on a local station or on cable, which is generally much less expensive and reaches people in your own community. When on the air, publicize your church. Make it a major objective to get the viewers to attend and become involved in your church. This is an excellent way to enlarge your relevance base.

The Internet

The Internet is an effective tool for enlarging the relevance base for your church. More and more people are capable of going on-line and finding your web page. Your message should be designed to meet their needs. The Internet is always available, twenty-four hours a day. If your church is not ready for its own web site, you might link your message with others. If you do so, be certain the sites you are linking with are "message friendly" with your church.

Remember, your objective is to interest people in attending and participating with your church. Don't scatter your image; focus on your image. Make your Internet statement a replica of who you are. Provide the current and active name, address, phone, fax, e-mail address, and other information for your church. People who view your web site should be able to locate or contact you.

Most congregations have members or people involved with the church who are capable of developing and placing your web message, people who specialize in creating and maintaining web sites. You may wish to use their services, but be careful you don't become unnecessarily connected with any ventures and products with which your message and program is not compatible. If you do not already have a web site or a link with another site, then appoint a committee to study this electronic opportunity. Talk with others who use the Internet successfully. Visit their web sites. The Internet is certainly one of the most creative and updated technologies to enlarge your base for relevance.

Please remember when I discuss these tools of communication, such as printed media, radio, television, and the Internet, that I fully recognize that these tools of communication are primarily used for the purpose of ministry to the needs of people. Your primary purpose is not to raise money. But this is a book on finding funds to support your ministry, and at the base of this challenge is finding prospects to solicit. These tools we have explored for enlarging your congregation may also help you enlarge the relevance base.

Information *my presentation*

The next phase in the anatomy of a gift is *information*. Having defined your institutional needs, developed your prospect list to underwrite those needs, and selected methods to expand your relevance base, you must inform the prospects as to what your needs are and how and when the prospects may provide funds to meet those needs.

The best ways of informing prospective donors are:

- pulpit presentations
- worship services' verbal and printed announcements
- church newsletter
- special mailings

- newspaper stories
- group events
- printed brochure
- printed question-and-answer pamplet
- video
- the Internet
- word of mouth

Announcements from the pulpit during a worship service are an excellent way to inform your congregation of a projected campaign. From time to time, use the pulpit and worship service to update the progress.

The church newsletter should be your regular voice to the congregation. It should announce a special appeal, how many dollars are needed, what the money will accomplish, the names of the leaders of the appeal, a projected calendar, announcements of upcoming events connected with the appeal, and a report of the events. As you will discover in later chapters, public announcements and information do not take place until after you have solicited the larger advance gifts from donors. This is especially true for a campaign to raise capital dollars for land, new buildings, etc. This timing is very important.

Special mailings, including a letter from the pastor and the basic information regarding the upcoming appeal, are a good method for getting out the information. It is usually wise to develop a name and logo for the campaign, including the list of the campaign leaders, on special stationery.

Newspaper stories are a good way to distribute information. Make sure your release times for stories do not conflict with the campaign plan. For example, if you publicly announce a capital campaign before you have time to cultivate and solicit your major donors, this may result in a reduced gift from some of these potential donors. As you will see later, every campaign must secure a certain percentage of its total goal from a few major gifts. If major gift prospects hear about this campaign before you have an opportunity to inform them of the need and cultivate them for the range of gifts needed, they may make an "average gift." People give against a goal. The donor may know the approximate size of the congregation and divide the goal by that number. Average giving, especially by the major gift prospects, will spell certain defeat for a fund-raising campaign. Take care to cultivate these potential major donors before beginning a general campaign.

Major gift donors often give against each other. If you publicize a smaller gift early in the campaign, the major donor may give against this standard. Later it may be hard to increase their commitment. Timing is important in releasing information.

Group event. You will best inform people in either group or individual settings, depending on the level of giving. For large gifts it is generally more successful to call on the donor prospect personally. The institutional leader, or pastor, along with one other person should make these visits. The next level of giving prospects may be informed in small group settings. This is preferably held in the leader's home. The rest of the donor prospects are informed in a large group setting, such as the church or a community meeting room. Often this is a dinner followed by an inspirational information presentation.

The brochure. Most fund-raising appeals have an informative and motivating brochure. A brochure in itself will not raise much money. It must be surrounded with events as part of a full campaign. The brochure should clearly present the need and describe how the need will be funded. If a building is involved in the campaign, the brochure should include pictures showing the need and architectural renderings illustrating how the need will be filled. It should provide a breakdown of the cost of the program or building project. It should include a message from the pastor or institutional leader and the names of the leaders supporting the appeal. The brochure need not be long (four to eight pages) and should have plenty of white space. It should be printed on good quality paper and have a self-cover, often including a picture. The back page is often the back cover and should include the name, location, phone, fax, and e-mail address of the church. The use of color is optional. You may create an attractive brochure with colored ink on a white or matching color stock paper. The size of the brochure is optional, although most brochures are 8½-by-11 inches. Have envelopes printed with a return address, and distribute the brochure with the matching envelopes. The brochure should sell your appeal in words, charts, and pictures.

The question-and-answer pamphlet is optional but is usually a very successful piece for informing prospective donors. This is usually a shortened version of the brochure, with no pictures, in a question-and-answer format. Think through the questions regarding needs, how many dollars are needed, how the need will be met in the appeal, and why the donor should give. The Q & A is generally a single-fold pamphlet on good paper stock in one color and should fit in a #10 (letter-sized) envelope. Your printed pieces should not be too expensive. If they are too elegant, donors may resist the appearance of contributions going for the purpose of costly production pieces. On rare occasions, I have been involved in creating a very expensive brochure. It paid off because of the unique donor prospect list, but this is not generally the case.

The video. Since most people have access to VCR equipment, a video is often used to enhance the brochure. Videos offer the dimension of sound and music, which adds a compelling element in dispensing the information. Make sure it is done with quality. You may have people in your church who are capable of creating a video. If not, consult a professional. The video should tell the story of the church's need and thus inspire contributions. It should not be more than ten to twelve minutes long. The video may be used in making appeals to individuals, small groups, and large meetings. Time the release of the video so that it has an element of newness and excitement to everyone who sees it.

Word of mouth. After all is said and done, the vital information for a church appeal will be made by someone talking with somebody else who is a prospect. Those telling the story must be well informed so that they will dispense accurate information in the most winsome manner. Training sessions for each level of the campaign are necessary.

Cultivation

Once you have determined the need, created a plan to implement the need with financial support, determined the list of prospects to underwrite the support, and informed the people in a proper and timely order, it is time to move to the next stage in the anatomy of a gift—*cultivation*.

To cultivate means to develop interest. This means that the right people have heard the appeal story and are being encouraged and persuaded to give.

The focus in the cultivation phase of the appeal relates to the size of the gift.

The *largest gifts* are usually cultivated one-on-one or by a very small team. The pastor, church leaders, and other top donors are the cultivation team. The best results usually occur when a team of two people meets with the large donor prospect to present the appeal. The printed and video materials may be used.

The *middle-range gifts* are generally cultivated in a small group setting. The video material is usually shown and the printed materials presented. The pastor and/or a church leader may make a verbal appeal.

The remainder of the congregation is generally cultivated at a large group event. The video is presented, the brochure and Q & A are distributed, and the leaders of the congregation make a verbal presentation.

Involvement

Let the donors feel an ownership in the fund-raising appeal. Many times a large gift is generated because the donor gets involved in planning the fund-raising events. Statistics indicate this phase of involvement is often key in the anatomy of a gift, especially a large one.

Solicitation and Follow-Up

Generally a gift is not given until it is asked for. Asking is important. Who does the asking is important, particularly for major gifts. Timing for asking is important. It should be within the time frame of the appeal and also when the donor is best able to respond.

The person making the appeal should be the same one who was primarily involved in cultivating the prospect. Remember, peers respond better to peers. This is particularly true with the major gifts.

Along with the request to contribute, which is the heart of the solicitation, the solicitor should have a commitment instrument for the prospect to complete and sign. This assures donors that their specific wishes will be followed. A pledge card is the best instrument for this purpose.

Courts have said that if a number of people sign the same type of appeal card, it indicates that the pledge was not taken under duress, as might be the case in a single letter of intent. The pledge card becomes "prime paper" and should be retained in a safe repository for several years.

Churches do not usually attempt to adjudicate unfulfilled pledges if the donors' situations have changed such that they no longer are able or willing to fulfill their pledges. However, if the pledge is large and the donor dies before fulfillment, the church may make a claim against the estate like any other outstanding bill. Whether to press forward with the fulfillment of the pledge will depend on the assets of the estate, the amount of the commitment (generally a major gift), and how far the church has moved forward with expenditures on the basis of the pledge.

A printed pledge card is suggested because a verbal commitment is not fully adequate. The cards give the church an accurate record of expectation of funds. They also protect the donors' understanding of their commitments. No one should ever be able to say that a donor's gift was different than intended. A standard pledge card, signed by the donor, will remove this possibility.

Many designs and styles for pledge cards are possible. I prefer that they not be too wordy. I like the card to say just what the donor wants to contribute. The sample pledge card suggested here contains all the necessary information. The pledge card should be printed on good stock and easily read. It should fit into a #9 envelope for return to the church. The card should usually be given to a donor prospect inside the envelope, for privacy's sake.

Here is a sample pledge card that is tested and usable.

LOGO	Name of donor and address	1. Pledge $_____ 2. Paid $_____ 3. Balance $_____

Out of my/our interest in raising $1,000,000 to achieve the goals of the "Let's Build the Church" Capital Campaign,

I/we commit _____($_____)

Payable as follows: $_____ $_____ $_____
                         weekly   monthly   annually

Or _____

Print Name _____ Date_____

_____
Signature
All gifts are tax deductible. Make checks payable to:

_____
Church Name

Note the box in the upper right corner of the pledge card. Figures should be entered as indicated, i.e., pledge, amount paid, and balance. The printed numbers are used as a process system in following up with the campaign pledge. The pledge card becomes the tracking instrument.

#1 Should be circled when the donor's acknowledgment letter has been sent.

#2 Should be circled when the pledge information has been transmitted to the church's financial record department.

#3 Should be circled when the financial department posts the pledge for collection. (This system of collecting is usually done on a routine basis when the donor is notified on the current status of his or her pledge.) This pledge card information will become the basis for a "tickler file" to turn the pledges into gifts.

Commitment

When the solicitation is made, the pledge card is handed to the donor prospects. It then becomes the donors' private option to complete the commitment. They should not feel pressured but made aware of the importance of the timing of the commitment. The solicitor should challenge donors to do their very best but should also respect whatever the donors decide. In many cases the commitment is made at the time of solicitation.

Commitment time is the most important in the anatomy of a gift. It should be serious, thoughtful, and prayerful. Everything leading to the moment of commitment should stress these principles. If too much pressure and hype is applied and the donors commit beyond their ability to fulfill, the church is faced with "shrinkage" in collections. On the other hand, if not enough challenge has been made, the donors are not faith driven in committing.

Acknowledgment

When a donor has made a commitment and the pledge card is returned to the church, the donor should get a letter of acknowledgment immediately. The letter should include a gracious "thank-you" and an accounting of the

76

amount of the pledge and how the donor indicated it would be paid. This information must be exactly as the donor has stated on the pledge card. If any payment has accompanied the pledge, that exact amount should be listed. This simple acknowledgment is sometimes not done properly or on time. This is a serious oversight.

Collection Procedures

Finally, the campaign effort then moves to *collection procedures* as established by the church. Every pledge must be treated with respect. All donors should be updated on the status of their pledge. They need this to motivate fulfillment of their pledge and for tax reasons.

The anatomy of a gift is very important to church fund-raising. These steps may vary some but not much. Each phase must be studied carefully and carried on in order and in a timely fashion.

5

RAISING FUNDS FOR THE ANNUAL BUDGET

If the congregation truly embraces the theology of giving, if the individual members manage their lives on the principle of Christian stewardship, and if each church member practices the tenets of tithing (giving at least 10 percent of his or her income for the Lord's work), then the problems of raising the funds necessary for meeting the annual budget are generally resolved.

However, this is not always the case. Statistics tell us that fewer than 5 percent of church donors actually tithe. The average donation by adults who attend Protestant churches is about seventeen dollars per week. In my own Presbyterian denomination, the average donation was twenty-two dollars per week in the year 2000. When I read this, I felt pretty good. My denomination was giving five dollars more per member per week than the other average Protestants. Then I looked at the numbers. Based on their average weekly gift, their average income (if they had been tithing) would have been under one thousand dollars per month. That's below the poverty level. Presbyterians on average are not living below the poverty level. Presbyterians are not tithing; neither are other Protestants or Roman Catholics. But we should keep preaching, teaching, encouraging, and practicing these tenets of tithing. A stewardship-driven church is a successful church, and stewards are growing, maturing Christians.

These underlying principles are the foundation for the whole structure of raising funds to run the church.

Fund-raising is only one side of the equation. How the church spends the funds it raises is equally important. The collective principle of stewardship of the whole congregation must be a constant concern. The church should spend its money wisely, efficiently, and prudently. Jesus' parable of the talents applies to the congregation as a unit as well as to the individual. The congregation must give a good accounting of the money it receives. This includes its budgeting, its budget servicing responsibility, and its reporting. A budget starts with listing the needs and projecting the expenses to fill the needs.

Creating the Annual Budget

How does a local church create a budget? Does the congregation raise its income and then prepare a budget to spend it? Or does the congregation create the budget and then seek the dollars to service it? Actually much of this is done together, but generally the preparation of the budget should precede the solicitation for funds. Otherwise the church won't take bold mission steps.

However, the church program should not be controlled by the church budget. The budget should be the means to the end and not the end itself. The budget should grow out of program needs; program needs should not be determined by the budget. If all the budget makers do is look at last year's budget and keep it the same or "cut a bit here and a bit there," the church will be on the road to certain decline. Maximizing services and programs, rather than minimizing expenses, should be the underlying guide in determining the fiscal policies of a congregation.

I heard of one church that sends a letter each year to each member of the congregation. The letter asks for ideas and suggestions on how the church can improve its ministry. These suggestions, along with the input of the pastor, the staff, the program leaders, and the officers, are all brought to the table. Then the budget is designed to meet the program needs.

A budget is a statement of expenses needed for a period of time. In most churches it is for one year. It becomes the road map for the journey of the church throughout the year. Once it is carefully prepared, approved, and adopted, it deserves and requires utmost respect and should be carried out during the entire year.

The church leadership prepares the budget after the programs have all been carefully reviewed and validated. How a congregation spends its money generally provides a good profile of the life and health of the congregation. Statistics show that the more a congregation gives away to viable and important mission causes outside its own operational needs, the more money it receives from the supporters. However, budget structuring begins with the dollars needed to operate the local church for the next year.

Budgeting for Good Leadership

At the top of the list of expenditures must be the salary packages for the pastor and staff. These paid leaders make the difference in the life of the congregation. I recall, as a young pastor, hearing the words of a very old and wise pastor. Describing his formula for a successful church, he emphasized leadership and people, not facilities. He would often say, "There's more in the man than in the land." Of course we amend that statement today to include men and women—all those who are called, trained, and committed to give continuing leadership to the church. Through their leadership, many are brought into a personal relationship with Jesus Christ. Through their leadership, children and young people are trained in the high spiritual principles of Christianity, prepared to affirm their faith, and confirmed into the body of Christ. Through their leadership, the membership is discipled through worship, studies, and fellowship. Through their leadership, the congregation is introduced to the large worldwide mission of the church and guided into involvement in far-reaching ministries. The pastor and staff's services to the kingdom are legion. They are indispensable to the fulfillment of the church. They are the core of the servants that make it all happen.

At the top of the budget, therefore, are the funds designated for the living expenses of the professional church workers. "The laborer is worthy of his wages" (Luke 10:7). We have made great strides over the last half century in recognizing the importance of this truth in managing the church. I remember the "poundings" that congregations used to bring to a new pastor and his family. Not the kind of "pounding" where a few power-driven and mean-spirited vigilantes beat up the pastor and his family with ugly words and spiteful charges. We don't need that in the church! I am referring to the "pounding" when the congregation surprised the pastor and his family with a "pound of this and a pound of that." They brought food and supplies to meet the pastor's need for provision. Their spirit was right but the system was limited. These "poundings" didn't reach the bar set for paying the laborer "worthy of his hire."

In those days the doctor and dentist often didn't charge the pastor and family for medical service. The grocer gave the pastor a discount for the goods he bought. Vendors of many products and services gave these same types of charitable courtesies to the pastor. Many may say, "Those were the good ole days." They were good in spirit, but the results were limited. Gradually the clergy have received recognition, income, and benefits that have lifted the position from "handouts" to worthy wages, but we have a long way to go. Providing funds for a strong church staff should be the highest priority in determining the church's annual spending.

Recently I met with a church and reviewed its annual budget of more than $5 million, not including building or endowment funds. Over 30 percent of the total budget went to mission causes outside the local church expenditures. In the remaining local operating budget of $3,750,000, nearly 75 percent went to leadership expenses. The caption in that budget category read, "The largest single investment we make as a congregation is providing for a strong church staff. While the ministry and mission of the church ultimately resides with the laypeople of the church, the staff persons teach, care for, work alongside of, and equip lay leaders for Christian life and service." This clear and eloquent statement puts the role of the leadership team in proper perspective. The number of dollars or the number on the staff is not the point. The same truth applies to any congregation of any size. Put the staff people first on the spending list; their services represent the categories that will bring more people and more money into the church. You get the biggest bang from the budget buck in staff expenditures. The church can increase the emolument package for the ordained staff personnel in many ways. For example, a generous housing allowance under the favorable conditions set by the IRS provides non-taxable income. Other avenues to consider include tax sheltered 403(b), IRAs, and other church-participating retirement benefits; denominational pension programs; providing enough overage funds to pay the social security; providing an auto or auto allowance for staff church usage; travel expenses and study enrichment program expenses; and health insurance to cover the staff member and family. The additional benefits over and above the salary should be a part of each congregation's leadership team financial support.

Every congregation should have a personnel committee. The committee's objective should not be to see how hard and how long they can work the staff for the minimum amount of compensation. Rather they should study the personal needs of their staff and the ways they may add to their comfort and vocational satisfaction.

Budgeting for Programs

The next item in the budget priority should be the dollars needed to operate the programs of the congregation. This item does not include personnel costs. In addition to program promotion, it includes information systems, printing, postage, supplies, and other expenses associated with communications for these ministries. The "separate" programs of the church are an integral part of the local ministry and should be the responsibility of the whole congregation and generally included in the church's annual budget. Many times, the groups within the congregation pay for most or some of their own expenses (for instance, a youth group may raise funds for a mission trip), not because they have to but because they want to for the health of their particular organization and the outreach of the church.

Budgeting for Facilities

Alongside program expenses are the facilities expenses. The buildings and grounds must be well maintained. It is wise for the annual budget to also include the studied costs of deferred maintenance. We all know that the sermon at the worship service may be terrific, the music magnificent, the physical setting beautiful, but if the heater isn't working on a cold day, the congregation shivers through the experience. Churches should budget adequate dollars for utilities, equipment, and repairs. The congregation should be informed of their costs. A wise congregation strives to create an endowment fund from which the income is designated to cover all or part of the buildings and grounds' maintenance and repairs. We will discuss creating an endowment fund in a later chapter. Using endowment income for these expenses frees more money for leadership and program expenses.

Budgeting for Church Giving

The working budget for a healthy congregation also includes thoughtful and generous gifts for ministries not included in the congregation's operational dollars. We formerly referred to this item in our budget as "benevolence." Not a bad term. It means charitable gifts of kindness. I guess we moved away from the term because we didn't want the recipients of our charity thinking that they were getting handouts. Mission giving is never a handout. Mission giving is responding to the call of Christ to share our love. This includes our money.

The churches that experience the greatest vitality and growth are churches that give high priority to mission giving. How much should that be? That varies with each congregation, as does where the mission gifts are given. Certainly if we advocate the tithing principle of 10 percent as the standard of giving for the individuals of the congregation, the church "mission" giving should be at least at that level. Many churches exceed that. I have worked with a number of churches that set a goal of giving 50 percent to missions. I've known churches that have a policy of giving one dollar away for every one dollar spent at home. Each congregation should set its own mission goal and strive to increase that portion of the budget each year until they reach it. A good place to start would be the tithe (10 percent). Work toward that standard and move beyond it as the Lord blesses.

The latest statistics from my own Presbyterian denomination are as follows:

	1995	2000
Average Contribution per Member	$813	$1154
Local Expenditures per Member	$736	$1056
Mission Expenditures per Member	$77 (9.5 percent)	$98 (8.5 percent)

The percentage decrease in mission giving represents a slight decrease in giving to the validated missions of the denomination. It also represents a slight increase to mission causes outside the denomination. Local congregations now tend to give more attention to mission causes outside their denomination because some of the mission causes seem more relevant and better managed.

Nondenominational churches have a variety of options for giving to missions. However it is done, a growing, dynamic church reaches out to others.

After adding all the expenditures, local and otherwise, the "needs package" is the budget. It raises the donor's consciousness. It highlights the priorities of the congregation. It informs the people and motivates them to step up and reach out.

Raising the Funds to Underwrite the Budget

Some churches do nothing but make their appeal for support and allocate the money as it comes in. They will say that they are living by faith. Much good can be said of that policy. If Christian stewardship is the driving force of the congregation, this hands-off policy has a much better chance of succeeding. Other churches will have an annual appeal season in which they inform the congregation of the needs for the next year and solicit pledges to underwrite those needs.

I have served churches with both those policies. I lean toward having a yearlong stewardship emphasis because it is vital to individual spiritual growth. I also advocate having an annual appeal, in order to inform the entire congregation of the real operational needs and the growing challenges of the church's mission. If you plan to have an annual appeal, make it a positive one. Of course, the key is a well-thought-out, prayerful, carefully prepared budget.

The next task is to develop a capable campaign team. I say "campaign" because it should have a definite target and a time frame for completion. The campaign team should be made up of people who:

- have vision;
- have personality appeal to communicate the vision;
- are team players;
- do not need the position for reasons of ego or to promote their own agenda;
- are able and willing to commit time to see the campaign to completion;
- show personal commitment to the church in attendance, giving, and service;
- are willing to be informed and take counsel from other church leaders, including the pastor; and
- have a positive profile in the congregation—the people respect them.

The pastor and select staff should also be on the campaign team to provide information and resources. The campaign team should set the campaign plan, materials, and events necessary to make it happen successfully.

An important factor to consider up front is the theme for the campaign. The theme should vary each year in order to reach the set goals and to make the campaign exciting. If the budget calls for a generous increase, the theme should reflect this need for increase in the appeal. I recall one church where I counseled on the annual stewardship campaign for several years. One year we really needed more per capita giving, so our theme was "Step up!" The brochure and other materials pictured a stairway with steps labeled "25 percent." We succeeded in raising the per capita giving by 25 percent. That theme was effective for that year. I recall another campaign where we needed more members to participate, so the theme for that campaign was "Be counted." Everything we said drove home the point that as members of the congregation each person owed it to themselves and the church to be counted with the others who make the church function.

After selecting the theme, consider the plans for information and cultivation.

1. Information

Informational letter. A general letter to the congregation, signed by the pastor and committee, and stating the theme, goal, and timing of the annual appeal.

Pulpit sermons. Sermons on stewardship should be given by the pastor, not only at campaign season but strategically placed throughout the year in order to develop the spiritual life of the church ministry. George Barna, in his book *How to Increase Giving in Your Church,* offers some penetrating statistics on this point:

- Churches in which pastors preach a single message about giving raise more money per capita than those churches in which no preaching about Stewardship takes place.
- Churches in which pastors preach two or more non-consecutive messages on the subject show more increase per capita giving over one sermon per year.
- Churches in which the pastor preaches two or more consecutive messages raise more money per capita than the singular message produces.
- Churches in which pastors preach two or more consecutive messages about Stewardship raise significantly more money per capita than do churches that hear two or more non-consecutive money messages.
- Churches in which pastors preach a series of messages about giving are nearly two and a half times more likely to experience an increase in giving than when preachers speak about it one sermon at a

time on two or more non-consecutive occasions during the year.[1]

These statistics should encourage a series of sermons in connection with the annual campaign appeal.

It is also helpful to have team members make brief informative statements during the worship services during three to four weeks of the annual appeal. These presentations must be carefully prepared and delivered with skill. If the church uses a large TV screen in worship, information and cultivation messages, carefully and persuasively done, may also be shown during the worship on several Sundays. Some churches use dramatic presentations to inform and cultivate the congregation. These should be carefully prepared and skillfully presented. Worship service bulletins are also effective in communicating stewardship needs and information. If possible, make the appeal in the form of an insert for the worship folder. It will not confuse the worshiper and also will provide something they may take home to think and pray about. The regular congregation newsletter should be used to inform the members. Other items that are helpful in informing and motivating congregations are:

Campaign brochures. They should be clearly printed on good stock. Pictures that represent new budget items are important. Charts and graphs that connect concrete numbers to the theme message are valuable. Brochures should be easy to read, with a balance of text, graphics, and white space.

Campaign questions and answers. There should be no more than ten questions relative to the campaign, with short and clear answers. They should be printed on good paper and sized to fit into a coat pocket or purse.

Campaign commitment card. A very important document that is considered prime paper for estate purposes.

It should not be too wordy and should have a space for the donor's name and a pledge box where the donor indicates the total commitment for the year and how he or she wishes to pay it. The card should include a place for the pledger's signature and date. Instructions should be included on how to write the checks, along with a note that all gifts are tax deductible. The pledge card should fit into a #9 return-addressed envelope. For privacy purposes, pledge cards should always be presented with a return envelope. The card and envelope will then fit into a #10 envelope, for mail solicitation with appeal letters. The pledge card envelope should have the name and address of the church printed on it for return. (See chapter 4 for more descriptions of pledge cards and all printed materials needed for campaigns.)

Video. Videos should be clear, short in duration, exciting, quality production. They are to be used for group cultivation events and possibly at a worship service. Don't overuse them, which can oversaturate the message.

2. Cultivation Events

Depending on the size of the church, the cultivation events may be a dinner or dessert meeting for the entire adult congregation:

- The size of the congregation will determine whether to conduct one or more church family events.
- Annual appeal campaign sessions should normally be held in the church facilities, if possible. Satellite cultivation events are sometimes needed.
- The program should be exciting, informative, persuasive, and not too long. Focus on the stewardship appeal. Do not discuss other church business. As a fund-raising principle, if you plan to ask atten-

91

dees to make a commitment at an annual appeal or capital campaign event, it's appropriate to tell them in the invitation or promotional material. Place a Q & A brochure at each table space.

- The video should inform and motivate the donors.
- The brochure with a pledge card inside the return envelope should be distributed toward the end of the program. The brochure should be a surprise to the viewers. A gifted team member should go through the brochure with the group.
- The final appeal to participate is given by the pastor or a gifted communicator on the appeal campaign team.
- Each attendee is asked to fill out the commitment cards. The person making the commitment appeal should explain the card so there will be no confusion.
- End with a brief interlude, perhaps with quiet music, for the people to discuss their commitment and sign the cards. They should all have been told prior to the event that they would have the opportunity to declare their commitment during the session. When the cards are completed, each is placed into the return envelope. One person at each table takes the cards forward, at the appropriate time, for the celebration of declaration at the commitment table. *Or,* each person is asked to take the Q & A, pledge card, and brochure home for prayer and study and return it to the church on Commitment Sunday.

This procedure eliminates the old "every member canvass," where committee members were given pledge cards for members of the congregation and asked to solicit their pledges. Instead, this solicitation process usually takes place after all the cultivation events are complete.

The "every member canvass plan" has not been very successful of late. Often the least persuasive people make the calls only because they are willing to serve, not because they are necessarily gifted in presenting the information.

I prefer an alternative to the "every member canvass plan" where certain preselected donor prospects are assigned to certain selected team members. These team members are selected on the basis of their giving record and involvement in the church. They are also selected on a financial peer basis, because this enables better communication. The team members do not solicit the pledges but do personally invite and motivate the selected donor prospects to attend the cultivation events. They also stand available to interpret the appeal and to answer questions. This special group feels responsible for the donor prospects' response in the event the prospects don't attend the cultivation event or are not present on Commitment Sunday. They serve as the follow-up team to complete the campaign. They should not be assigned more than three or four names each.

Some churches use a final telephone appeal to non-participants before concluding the appeal. This is sometimes not very successful, especially if the larger donor prospects already have been assigned to team members for follow-up.

Following the receipt of the pledge cards, all communication with donors should include these suggestions:

- All pledgers should receive a letter of acknowledgment for their commitment, with the amount and payout plan stated exactly as the pledge card has directed.

- All pledgers should receive offering envelopes.
- Pledge cards should be kept in a safe repository.
- All pledge information should be posted for every donor, with collection procedures established for tabulation.
- All pledge participants should be sent a semiannual report on the status of their pledges.
- All donors should be sent a year-end statement of all gifts received for the year. This is important for IRS purposes.

Stewardship Education

Annual support of the congregation is extremely important in order to develop the spiritual life of each member and to generate funds needed to operate the church and its mission. Support for the church should not be optional. The amount of the contribution may vary according to ability and circumstance, and all gifts should be highly respected.

The stewardship system should:

- begin with the Christian education curricula for children and youth.
- be a vital part of the new members class preparing for church membership.
- be put in written form and approved by the officers of the congregation and distributed to each member.
- include an occasional review of all members' giving records. Those who never support their church should be given an opportunity to declare their intention as in any other organization.

Of course, we are dealing with the members of the body of Christ. We must be understanding, sensitive, and alert to all conditions. But we owe it to each member to let them know that we care about them. Our caring includes their spiritual life and growth. Their spiritual life includes their stewardship.

Everybody can give something. A prayer and a token gift may be all some members can do. They should be made to feel good about their participation. Jesus praised the poor widow woman who gave the two mites (Luke 21:2). Of course you cannot build big buildings and promote great programs with mites, but you can build good people who give all they can.

Gifts are important in both quantity and quality. All we should ask is for each member to do his or her best. The church should expect that. If that is done, the bills will be paid, the buildings and grounds will be built and maintained, and the mission of the whole church will be enlarged.

Stewardship is the catalyst!

6

MEETING THE
CHALLENGES OF A
GROWING CHURCH

A growing congregation fulfills the command of going into all the world—especially your world—with the gospel.

That is what the Great Commission is all about.

As I watched churches over the past fifty years as a pastor, a denominational administrator, and a consultant to congregations of all sizes, traditions, and locations, I have observed some basic trends and conditions among all congregations. Unless the church is located in one of the few areas in the country where there is no population growth or even decline, most congregations must be "growth driven." I have observed that those congregations who do not grow begin to die. Of course plateaus and leveling in the growth pattern will occur, but any church in a developing area must grow in order to survive.

It's a mathematical equation. Church members die, move away, or change church relationship. They must be replaced, or in time there will be no congregation. In order to survive, a congregation must grow. Growth creates problems, and many of these problems require dollars to overcome.

Before we tackle the challenge of providing program space and dollars for growing congregations, let us look briefly at those churches that are not experiencing growth and may even have population loss. These churches have serious planning to do for the life of the congregation. After careful studies of the trends and demographic facts, the dying congregation must consider the following options:

- Relocation
- Merger with another congregation serving the same geographical area, maybe even if the other congregation is outside your denomination. That label may not be as important today as before. I know of many mergers that have been successful and created new life and growth for the merged congregations.
- Simply stay put and design a quality program for the spiritual life of each congregant until there are no more sheep to shepherd.

Whatever the course chosen, even the small church must face up to its future and define goals and objectives for its remaining life. Small churches need great help and attention. Even the church in demise has served a great purpose. It has finished its course. That dignity of service must be preserved in some way. A strong growing church can adopt the remnant of the dying church. Each is blessed by what the other brings to the table in tradition or energy.

Now back to our primary concern of growing churches. How do we handle a growing congregation? Growth brings excitement. Greater numbers attend. Increased program activities and even crowded conditions give a lift and vigor to a congregation. But problems often begin with growth. For instance, not all the members of the congregation may want the church to grow. They are content with the status quo. They do not want to surrender their leadership or share the future of the church with newcomers. This attitude may become the basis for serious divisions within the congregation.

When I served as an executive for the presbytery of Los Angeles, we were busy planning and organizing new churches. Those churches are today among the largest and most vigorous in the area. But growing has been difficult. For example, we expected dissension in a new church within one and a half to two years of organization. The problem was growth. Sometimes the dissension became nasty church fights. Often it could be narrowed down to the original start-up group who could not gracefully share their leadership power. In the beginning days, the members of the steering committee developed a great deal of esprit de corps. They were motivated to get a church started and worked hard and faithfully. Had it not been for their commitment and arduous efforts, the congregation might have never happened. Their very success in developing more people to start the church became their frustration. As the church was organized and charted, new people were elected to share leadership, along with the beginning group. This is where the problems began.

I noticed that trouble usually took the form of an antipastor movement. The reason for this was obvious.

99

The pastor was committed to growth, which meant bringing new people into the congregation. This took his time away from the original leaders, creating frustration among them. They felt they had lost their pastor. They would never say this, however; rather they would complain that the pastor was no longer available. That his sermons were not as good. That he didn't keep confidences as he once did. He just wasn't the same anymore. What they were really saying was, "We are frustrated and don't want to grow. We don't want to surrender our leadership role." The situation and feelings became divisive.

I remember one congregation where this leadership frustration had reached a point of pending disaster. As the executive for churches in the area, I met with various churches' officers to hear their complaints. We took all the information, together with a full report of the pastor and his supporters. On some occasions it seemed better to recommend the pastor relocate to an area where his gifts would be of greater value. In other cases it seemed prudent to temporarily dissolve the leadership boards until a less stressful environment prevailed. Time can be a great healer. At this particular church, we had called a congregational meeting immediately following the Sunday morning worship services to receive the report, which was to recommend that the pastor be relocated and a new pastor called. I was the pulpit guest for that worship service. Following the worship, I was to preside at the congregational meeting and make the report.

I went to the podium to call the meeting to order. I heard shouting from the congregation and physical movement going on. I tried to call the group to order, but they wouldn't quiet down. I realized I was hearing furious argument, and one of the loudest voices came from a man who had been a leader in getting the church started. He was having problems with the church growing, and he was losing leadership and power. He wanted the pastor to relocate, but he was so caught up in his enmity that he wouldn't wait for the announcement confirming his hope. Instead his shouting was disrupting the opening prayer and call to order for the meeting. I finally got the group's attention and told them this little parable: "There were five crows sitting on a pump handle. They had all eaten their capacity of prunes. One crow flew off the pump handle fifteen yards north and dropped dead. One flew fifteen yards south and dropped dead. One flew fifteen yards east and one flew fifteen yards west and both dropped dead. There was one crow left on the pump handle and he flew fifteen yards straight up in the air and dropped dead." I then said, "The moral of this story is, don't fly off the handle when you're full of prunes." The perpetrator of the argument stormed out of the meeting. However, that bit of humor brought the rest of the meeting together. Surrendering some leadership when the body is growing is often very difficult. I've noticed this not only with new congregations but also with established congregations. When a new pastor or other congregational and staff leaders come to an established church and precipitate growth, some of the people within the congregation resent the growth; trials begin and growth is stifled.

What do you do when those who do not want the church to grow are fracturing the spirit of the congregation? To begin with, you love them. You recognize what leadership they have given in the past and praise them for their contributions. You also recognize that the church may be growing beyond their leadership ability, which frustrates them. For psychological and spiritual reasons, they should take a moratorium on their leadership position. Such a move will enable the church to move forward with growth and development and give new leaders opportunity to serve. It is sometimes wise to make leadership changes before proceeding with fund-raising campaigns. This may take some time, prayer, and loving, careful handling, but it is worth it if the church continues to grow to capacity.

Creating a Vision Initiative Group

Having acknowledged the need for growth and developed a consensus within the congregation to grow, it is now necessary to create a planning committee that will carefully look at all the growth requirements, including space and programs, and report back to the congregation for action. I like to call this committee the vision initiative group. Vision—because they are seeing into the future. Initiative—because they will be taking the first steps to make something happen to meet the needs for growth.

This group is appointed to study seriously all the growth patterns and future needs of the congregation. It should base its mandate upon facts, figures, demographic studies, trends inside the congregation, and needs within the community. Personalities or congregational politics should not drive the agenda or actions of this group. The prime purpose for the vision initiative group is to study the church's activities and space requirements and to recommend a solution for the needs caused by the growth.

The vision initiative group should be sanctioned by the highest body or board within the church. Its findings should eventually go to the entire congregation for action when appropriate. Therefore it must have the most serious appointment and support and should not be treated only as an ad hoc discussion group.

Each department of the church should be represented in the vision initiative group, and when possible, the chairperson or leader of each program group should be officially selected to serve on the committee. The group should include:

1. Senior pastor
2. Pastoral and office staff as selected
3. Representative of the:
    a. Children's ministries
    b. Youth ministries
    c. Young adult ministries
    d. Senior ministries
    e. Family ministries
    f. Women's ministries
    g. Men's ministries
    h. Music and worship ministries
    i. Outreach ministries
    j. Charitable ministries
    k. Buildings and grounds ministries
    l. Other ministries
4. Representatives at large from the congregation, including:
    a. Financial leaders
    b. Philanthropic leaders (It is very important to have some people writing the agenda for action who are capable of underwriting it.)

The vision initiative group should be large enough to cover all the need bases but of a manageable size to generate action. The number will depend upon the local congregation.

A chair and possible cochair should be appointed or elected, who will carefully call the group together and moderate the agenda. These people should be highly respected and influential within the congregation, have a broad overview of the life of the congregation, give evidence of leadership, and be able to communicate effectively and interpret the action of the vision initiative group.

The agenda should begin where the church is in the moment of time that they first meet. Here are the questions to be considered for the first meeting:

1. What are the strengths and weaknesses of the congregation?
2. Who is the church serving? Define the problems that have arisen. Grade the effectiveness of service for each group within the congregation.
3. What is needed to serve the congregation more effectively?
4. What is needed for the church to serve more effectively in the community?
5. What are the space needs for the present programs?
6. What is the attitude of the congregation for missions outside the community?

These questions should all be studied carefully, along with any other ministry needs. The representation from each department should bring to the table the successes, problems, needs, and anticipations within its own program. Time must be allowed to study each need separately. Time is necessary to do a thorough job of exploring the needs. Sometimes many meetings will be necessary. Set a time to start and adjourn each meeting. Stay within the timetable.

Once the needs are placed on the table, they should be evaluated and placed in a priority order. This is sometimes the trickiest part of the whole procedure and requires prayer, negotiation, and agreement. Finally, a line of action is developed to present the vision initiative to the congregation.

Many of the needs will fall into the categories of program development, management oversight, and leadership directives. Careful control and organization will help meet many of these needs. Some needs are space centered and may require more property, more buildings, and more building alterations. Overcrowding is generally at the base of space needs. Too many people are attending to fit into the rooms that the church has on campus.

Facility Needs

The first thing to do is consider space management for the existing rooms and facilities. Are they all being used to maximum efficiency? Can activities be combined? Have some activities reached the point where the space demand for their program is no longer pressing? Can these programs be terminated without hurting the fellowship and spiritual development of that special group? After all these adjustments have been made and the congregation is still growing and meeting places and parking lots are full, what can the church do?

At this point the vision initiative group is faced with some options:

- Repair and upgrade the existing facilities to develop more space.
- Add on to the existing buildings by attaching laterally or adding space vertically on top of existing buildings.
- Purchase property contiguous to or nearby the current site.

105

- Keep the current site. Purchase and develop another site. Create two campuses.
- Sell the current site and relocate.

Each of these alternatives has possibilities and should be considered in light of all the facts and numbers, together with the morale and enthusiasm of the congregation. Finally, what do the demographic statistics reveal? Let's consider the alternatives in reverse order.

Relocation

This is the most drastic of all the options. However, sometimes it is the best. It generally is done as a last resort but should be considered early, if the other alternatives are not really options. Relocating a congregation requires careful consideration.

1. What will happen to the current membership? Will they move gracefully? Will the new location make it too difficult to attend the services and church activities? A study of the membership's residential geography, transportation systems, and ability to change is very important. It is understood that a few who have strong emotional ties to the current campus will have difficulty accepting the relocation move. These people should be considered but should not be the sole determining factor.
2. Will the new location be acceptable to most of the congregation?
3. Will the prospective new location allow for growth and development for forty years or more? The vision initiative group should think in such long-range terms.

106

4. What are the demographics for the new site? Is the new site located where new people will reside?
5. Are other churches in the location already serving the community well? Will the new site simply make you competition, or is there room for your congregation and the existing churches? Are your programs and emphases distinct enough that you will have a significant niche for community ministry?
6. Would your church bring special service and importance to the life of the new community?
7. What are the community services such as schools, parks, and recreation? Would the community leaders welcome you?
8. Have you a significant group in your current church family who will serve as a core group in the new location?
9. Is appropriate property available? Is the property highly visible? Is the property accessible to traffic flow? Can people get to the site freely, comfortably, and safely? Does the site have plenty of parking space available? What about additional parking space as the church grows and programs increase over the next forty years?
10. Can the congregation afford it? In most places land is very expensive, particularly large parcels. I recommend you acquire capital for land acquisition before you move the congregation. Then use the proceeds from the sale of the current campus and a second capital building-fund campaign for buildings. Some borrowed funds may be used for the building and ground improvement on the new site.
11. Many times the relocation to a more favorable site will turn the church from a community to a regional church. The congregation will want to study models of regional churches and be excited and motivated by what they see. The relocation

often becomes the catalyst for a megachurch. This could be your future if you decide to relocate. Do you want this? This is a key question.

If all these studies have been made thoroughly and the relocation plan seems feasible and achievable, then the church should proceed to make the bold move. These steps may require:

- approval of the congregation;
- approval of the governing ecclesiastical authority, above the congregation, where that is necessary;
- indication that the church can receive use permits and building permits from the civic authorities for the new site; and
- funding lined up for purchase.

Relocation is not a simple thing. It should be undertaken with great care after all considered points are a go. Then go for it!

A Second Campus

Sometimes all these studies will indicate the church must relocate in order to provide growing space. However, because of the attachment of congregational members to the current location and its easy access, the church has a difficult time in deciding on relocation and the possibility of cutting off some members or feeling that they are forsaking their mission to the area in which they have served for many years. The solution to this situation may be to consider a second campus. Colonial Presbyterian Church in Kansas City, Missouri, made the decision to keep their current campus of 17 acres, with little room for building expansion and parking spaces, and purchased a second site of 129 acres about one mile away. The second campus is in the state of Kansas but in a dynamic growing area. The new location met all the criteria for future expansion and community service.

A quiet appeal was made to selected prospects, and we raised the funds to buy the land. We conducted a building-fund campaign, which generated the funds to start the construction of the first all-purpose building on the campus.

Following the land acquisition, the church started Sunday worship services in a private Catholic high school auditorium located near the campus. Several families of the original Colonial congregation became the core group for the new congregation. Both congregations were under the same organizational structure and served by the same pastoral staff.

Purchase Property

Another alternative is to acquire property contiguous or very near the existing church campuses. This may cost a lot of money and requires careful strategy. If there is vacant land next to your church—buy it!

Hopefully you will have a relationship with the owner or an opening for dialogue. If the property is improved, with buildings or houses, your problem is larger.

When I served as Dr. Robert Schuller's assistant at the Crystal Cathedral, my primary role was development, which is an all-inclusive term for fund-raising. However, it also included campus development and property acquisition. The Crystal Cathedral needed more space for parking and buildings but wanted to remain in the same location. All usable ground space was occupied. The only alternative was property acquisition.

Adjacent to the church campus was five acres that included a number of dilapidated and overcrowded fourplex apartments. We purchased the property, even though we had to pay a heavy price for land we knew we must have.

All of the fourplexes were rented to low-income tenants. We agreed to help them all relocate. Finally the apartments could be torn down or removed for relocation. We ended up donating them to the municipality, who relocated them on a much less-expensive property. They renovated each apartment and provided rentals for low-income people.

Running through the land was a cement flood-control channel. It was filled with trash and of no value. We covered the channel according to the specifications and were able to put a road and paved parking spaces on the covered land. It was an expensive project, but it provided more usable land.

Finally we had five-plus useable acres. On it we built a 150,000-square-foot family life center building for schools, offices, and recreational centers.

It costs money and takes time to acquire property connected to the church campus, but it is worth it if there are no other alternatives.

At the same church we went through the process of acquiring many single-family homes in order to create space for parking and a much-needed international visitors center. This space was occupied by about fifty modestly priced tract houses. We began acquiring them one by one. The more we acquired, the higher the sales price became. By the time we finally bought the last house, the price had multiplied many times its true value for property in the area. But since it was up against the church property, we paid the premium price. This opened the needed space for the erection of the visitors center and parking spaces. It cost a great deal of money and a great deal of time to acquire property contiguous to the church but it was worth it. The church was able to remain in the same desired location.

Add On or Upgrade

If all studies indicate it is best for the church to stay at its same location and if more room is needed for parking and additional structures, the only alternative solution is to go up higher with high-rise parking facilities and construct taller buildings for activities. This may be restricted by the municipality coding for height limitation. Sometimes it is possible to add space on top of existing buildings. This requires careful engineering studies to be certain that the existing facility will carry the load of the additional construction.

The church's buildings might also be repaired, upgraded, or renovated to provide for additional program space.

After all the needs facing a growing congregation are clearly understood, the church should proceed with the best option.

- Repair, upgrade, or add on to the existing buildings.
- Purchase property near the church for more construction.
- Purchase property away from the existing property and start a "second campus" congregation.
- Purchase new property, sell the old property, and relocate the church.

Each of these options requires care, patience, and faith. It means change. These thoughts come from my good friend Jess Moody. He includes them in his lectures on church growth. They furnish good counsel and guidance for facing congregational changes connected with church growth:

One of the most important elements of church growth is change—not just accepting it, but embracing it. Here are sixteen undeniable truths about making change happen at your church:

1. Almost all leaders want to move faster than the rest of the organization.
2. Your potential opposition will show up within eight to twelve months.
3. Most people can handle no more than three major changes or four minor changes per year.
4. Make no more than two major and three minor changes per year.
5. Make certain that the two changes are major, vitally germane to the growth of the organization.
6. The major change will take two to four years to integrate into the organization, from top to bottom.
7. In presenting change, use common words. Don't make them learn a new vocabulary. (Executives love to use the word "paradigm." Down-the-liners hate it.)
8. People will adapt to a change if they understand that what they are getting is better than what they have to give up.
9. Leaders should let the organization's people know that change is hard for leadership too.
10. Don't announce change before you have sold your core group. Sell the center and the circumference will follow.
11. Show by projection how much better things will be five years from now.
12. Project how bad, or slowed down, things will be if the change is not effected.
13. Change is a good time for staff realignment, unless

the realignment will cut down too much on the acceptance of the change.

14. Space your changes at least four months apart.
15. Does the particular change build faith, instill hope, and demonstrate love?
16. Salt is a change agent. Jesus said, "You are the change agents of the world." So change it![1]

7

RAISING CAPITAL
FUNDS

After the vision initiative group has made its carefully
prepared report and the congregation has declared its
readiness to move forward with growth plans, the
church is ready to begin the fund-raising process. A committee should be appointed to study the costs of the
options selected for the growth plans and determine the
actual overall costs.

Acquiring property requires the counsel of a competent real estate resource. Upgrading or reconfiguring
existing facilities or building new ones requires the
counsel of a competent architect. Construction requires
the counsel of a contractor to furnish cost estimates.
Finally, money will be needed to finish and furnish the
project. Once all these dollar estimates have been studied, an overall goal is determined.

In many cases these dollars represent new construction costs. Generally these new buildings represent future activity centers for worship, education, recreation, and fellowship. When a building is completed, the operational and maintenance costs will begin. Ongoing heating and cooling, lights, power, water, and other recurring building operational costs must be budgeted. After opening the new facility, it won't be long before repairs will need to be made. Where will these extra expenses come from? If they are placed in the regular operating budget, it will mean the absolute necessity for more funding or some of the programs and ministry items in the budget will take a cut. It cannot be both ways.

I recommend that a 10 percent figure be added to the dollar goal of the capital campaign. This 10 percent will go into an endowment fund designated for maintenance and repairs, and the income from the corpus will be restricted for this purpose.

Once all these cost factors have been determined, it is time to add them all up and establish an overall goal or amount needed. Do not set a campaign goal yet, and do not "go public" with this cost figure yet. Other steps are necessary first.

Step number one is to establish a capital campaign team. This should be made up of some of the most successful, high-energy, large-thinking, and fund-raising types in the congregation.

- They should be people of highest integrity and credibility.
- They should be highly respected within the congregation and the community.
- They should be supportive of the pastor, staff, and programs of the church.

- They should be practicing stewards.
- They should be regular church attenders.
- They should be people of "high profile" in the congregation and community.
- They should be "centers of influence."
- They should be good listeners.
- They should be good with details and timetables and know how to get things done.
- They must be committed to attend the team meetings and commit the time it will take to get the job done.
- They should be good team players. It cannot be a "one-man show."
- Some should be church officers.
- Some should be good public speakers and skillful communicators.
- Some must be among the larger potential donors to the campaign. It is vital that some of the people who are creating the capital campaign are capable of contributing a large part of it.
- All should have a positive spirit toward the direction in which the church is moving and be highly supportive of the pastor, staff, and officers.

This capital campaign team is one of the most important factors in the success of the appeal. This profile of team candidates is challenging but achievable. Take time to do it well. Depending on the size of the church, some staff may be included on the campaign team. Their input will be important. If a staff person is administrating the business affairs, he or she should be on the team. The pastor should definitely be on the team but not as the chairperson.

The pastor may call the first team meeting together and introduce the purpose of the group. A chair, cochair, and secretary should be appointed or elected.

A capital campaign requires astute planning, constant direction, and supple management.

The first agenda item for the team is whether the congregation will need to seek outside help. This is always a big question: "Should we seek professional help to direct our campaign?" The size of the campaign and the potential complexities in reaching the goal will be determining factors in answering this question. Professional counsel will cost money. Every dollar that is spent on securing the campaign funds is theoretically one dollar less in funds to spend. On the other hand, if the professional fund-raiser will help you get more money, then it is a wise expenditure. Professional fund-raisers are helpful because:

- they have the *time* to give the direction needed to see to the small details that make for success.
- they have the *training* to know how to get the greatest response from the donors.
- they have the *talent* to persuade contributors.
- they have the *temperament* to do what is needed to accomplish the mission.

Many times the professional can say things and suggest methods of giving that would be hard for the pastor or other congregational leaders to say because of their subjective involvement.

The church leaders should take time in selecting a professional firm. Such firms vary in experience, skills, and price for their services. Some may function as brokers for their services. The actual person "directing" the campaign may be inexperienced and untrained, although the campaign firm may be prominent. The local congregation should insist on knowing the person and credentials of the individual actually directing their campaign. Some campaign organizations may have a template approach to fund-raising—"one size fits all." While certain steps are necessary for every campaign, the composition of the individual church must be studied and put at the very center of the timing, strategy, and "personality" of the campaign appeal. The professional director must be willing to recognize congregational differences and adjust to the uniqueness of the church's situation. A capital campaign is not a "cookie-cutter" program.

A congregation usually must pay a fee for these professional services. How much? This is a critical question and is usually determined by the amount to be raised, the amount of time it will take to raise it, and the experience of the professional.

Although the professional costs represent a percentage of the dollars to be raised, a percentage amount should not be the prime factor in determining the fee. In earlier days of professional fund-raising, the percentage fee structure was common. This led to questionable compensation. The professional fund-raiser would sometimes secure what came to be called "street corner pledges." The pledges were not reliable and the "shrinkage" factor in dollar collection was great. The fund-raiser had taken his fee on a percentage of money pledged and moved on to the next campaign, leaving the church holding the empty bag of uncollectible commitments. The accepted standard today is that a professional fund-raiser should base a fee for services rendered on a certain dollar amount.

Remember, the professional brings time, training, talent, and temperament to the campaign table. Along with these factors he must bring fund-raising wisdom and ability to counsel. The professional should be a proven and consistent leader, not someone who merely delivers a "canned" approach that may have worked before. It takes persistent and creative direction to lead each campaign.

Although professional fees should not be arrived at on a percentage basis, and there are many proven and reliable reasons for this, when the books are closed on a fund-raising campaign, clearly a percentage of the total was paid for professional direction and a percentage for other campaign expenses. Appropriate percentages vary with the size of the campaign. Although these figures cannot be "set in cement" because of local circumstances and changing fiscal times, a reasonable professional fee will be in the area of 5 percent, and the expenses for the entire campaign, including travel, events, materials, and promotion, will total no more than 10 percent. Certain campaigns with high media costs and promotion will exceed these percentages. But this is a good starting point and a reliable cost platform.

A number of individuals and firms offer professional fund-raising services. Some have more experience and proven results than others. Some charge a much higher fee than others. If your church decides to use outside counsel, take time to carefully check out their success record and credentials and be willing to negotiate the fee structure.

Over the past few years, I have worked with churches that have had a full-time campaign director but not a professional or firm. They have carefully gone through their own membership and found a layperson, usually recently retired and not dependent on job income, who had leadership qualities and people skills and who could be trained in the details of campaign direction. I have met with them and generated a detailed agenda for each step in the campaign. In addition to being enthusiastic, on the job, and willing to take direction, they still remained when the campaign was completed and could follow up with the collection procedures. An outside campaign organization is limited at this point because they have moved along to the next campaign. Your own "in-house director" remains on the job and may be vital in giving direction to the next phase or a new campaign.

Whatever your church decides, if you hire an outside professional, and I would frequently recommend this, when the professional firm is selected, the congregation should be prepared to respect their leadership, trust their judgment, and follow their counsel. I have met people along the "campaign trail" who have had a little fund-raising experience but not enough; they became a real source of difficulty in getting the job done. If you hire a professional, then let the professional lead and expect their leadership.

The rest of this chapter will be for those congregations who may not hire a professional and need to know the steps that a competent professional will use to make a campaign happen.

A Capital Campaign

First, *the capital goal should be determined*. This is best determined by the genuine needs package. There are various suggestions on the ratio of the campaign goal to the church's annual budget. Generally the campaign goal should be in the range of two to three times the average annual budget for the past three years. This is a start but should not be the major criteria for goal setting. Goal setting should grow out of the needs package. The needs must be bona fide. That is why we recommend such careful studies before launching a competent campaign, studies accomplished by the vision initiative group.

Second, *create a "gifts needed" chart*. This is like a road map for getting to your goal. It is one of the most important steps in developing a successful campaign. You have probably heard of the 80–20 rule, which states that 20 percent of the people give about 80 percent of the dollars in most appeals. That figure has some credibility but cannot be used as a firm base in determining the sources for gifts. This broad 80–20 gauge must be refined. Generally the "gifts needed" chart for a capital campaign will develop as follows:

- The top single gift should represent about 10 percent of the campaign target.
- The top ten gifts should generate between 45 to 55 percent of the target.
- The balance of gifts needed will be charted by categories of gifts.

These are not absolute figures but a reliable starting point. This chart is frequently called a "standard chart" because it sets the standard of what it will take to get the job done. It's hard to get there without it. Using a campaign goal of around $1 million as an illustration, let us look at a standard chart (or "gifts needed" chart) that was actually developed for a capital campaign. The goal grew out of the studied needs. If this campaign had been $10 million or $50 million, similar percentages in gift categories would have been created as the standard. The dollar amounts would vary, as would the number of donors.

A moderate-sized congregation had come up with needs of $1.2 million, including money for mission causes outside the capital needs and an additional 10

percent for endowment to service the cost of facilities'
maintenance and repairs.

The first standard chart developed looked like this:

GOAL: $1,200,000

Number of Gifts Needed	Amount of Gift	Total	Accumulative
1	$250,000	$250,000	$250,000
1	$100,000	$100,000	$350,000
3	$50,000	$150,000	$500,000
5 (10)	$30,000	$150,000	$650,000 (54%)
7	$25,000	$175,000	$825,000
10	$10,000	$100,000	$925,000
20 (47)	$5,000	$100,000	$1,025,000 (85%)
30	$3,000	$90,000	$1,115,000
60 (137)	$1,000	$60,000	$1,175,000 (98%)
Many gifts below	$1,000	$25,000	$1,200,000 (100%)

Number of giving units in congregation: 250.

The parentheses in the left column represent the
cumulative number of gifts needed up to that level.

The parentheses in the far right column represent the
percentage of the goal met to that level.

The Feasibility Study

If a professional fund-raising company is being used,
they will often do a feasibility study before entering the
contract. The final goal will be determined from the feasibility study. For our purpose here, we will assume that
the congregation directs its own campaign. In that case
a feasibility study will be conducted in order to get a fix
on whether the campaign is timely. Since the study is a
fact-finding process, it also becomes a vital cultivation

exercise. The people who are going to be asked to support the campaign later are given a voice in whether the campaign should be conducted.

The study is a survey form. The prospects selected for the interview include:

- pastor
- staff
- key officers
- select department leaders
- major donors of record
- major donor prospects with little or no major giving record
- community leaders who might be affected

This survey list should number from fifteen to thirty, depending on the size of the congregation. The people being interviewed should know why they are being asked for their opinion. Carefully construct and script the interview questions. Interviews should not last more than thirty minutes and should be conducted by appointment. If possible, try to schedule the interviews in a central location such as the church.

The key questions for each interview should be:

- Is the general health of the congregation good? What are your thoughts?
- Is the church growing?
- Are the needs being considered viable? (Name priorities of the needs package.)
- Is the church on the cutting edge of ministry in the community?
- Is the professional leadership of the church well accepted?

- Is the general church spirit right for a campaign to raise money for these needs?
- If motivated, will the people give above their regular support gifts to meet these special needs?
- Do you think we can get gifts in these gifts-needed ranges? (Here display the standard chart.)
- Do you see your commitment possible and the possible range of your gift?
- Would you pray about your role in the campaign?

The survey answers are tabulated, evaluated, and carefully studied in light of the needs package. If the consensus is positive toward moving forward, then the next step is to set the working target for the campaign. I like the word *target* rather than *goal* at this time. A *goal* may give the impression of completion. The survey may show that the timing is not right for the complete appeal to be undertaken. So a target is set.

The Campaign Target

Sometimes the campaign target may include funds for mission projects outside the "needs package," which is frequently brick and mortar. While this desire is admirable and consistent with the stewardship concept, it may not be timely to conduct both appeals together. Such an effort may become confusing and fracture both the needs-package appeal and the mission appeal. This is similar to using a "dual pledge card" for people to make commitments to the building fund and the operating fund on the same card. Wisdom exists in focusing on these internal needs separately. The theory behind coupling requests for missions with requests for capital funds is that it gives the donor prospect an option. That is exactly what it does, and both appeals may suffer. If the capital needs are real, then seek those funds and conduct the mission appeal separately. I know of several successful congregations who conduct several separate appeals each year. The congregation recognizes these appeals and selects to support those needs that interest them.

When the target is set, then it is time to tailor the "gifts needed" chart. In the case of our earlier model chart, the church conducted a feasibility study and found they should reduce the target to $950,000. A new chart was created using similar percentage factors. The campaign seemed achievable, and the results overpledged the target.

The Campaign Plan

- The target is stated and approved.
- The case statement for the appeal is created.
- A campaign theme is determined, along with the campaign logo.
- A campaign timetable is established and should include three divisions.
  1. Leadership gifts: for gifts above the top line on the standard chart (This is the first level of appeal.)
  2. Major gifts: for gifts in the second level of the standard chart (above the second line)
  3. General gifts: for gifts in the third and fourth levels of the standard chart (below the second line)

Prospective cultivating and soliciting is best done one level at a time, and the approved timetable must be respected throughout the entire campaign.

In capital campaigning, it is extremely important to go after the larger gifts first and to follow the appeal in the order of the standard chart. If the appeal is made one level at a time, the giving will reflect ability within that level. Finally, large gifts will inspire and lift small gifts, but small gifts will not lift large prospects. Timing for each solicitation level is therefore critical.

The Campaign Team

The campaign team should include officers:

1. General chairperson
2. Cochair
3. Secretary
4. Treasurer
5. Division chairs, one leader per campaign division
6. Represented staff, including senior pastor
7. Members-at-large who have capacity to give larger gifts
8. Campaign director (professional or nonprofessional)

Campaign Materials Needed

1. Feasibility summation statement
2. Case statement
3. Photos and renderings
4. Pledge card(s)
5. Question-and-answer booklet
6. Brochure
7. Video
8. Cultivation materials
9. Signs and banners
10. Collection system

Donor Prospects

1. *Leadership gifts.* Source: church members, giving records, former campaign(s), community, and friends
2. *Major gifts.* Source: same as leadership gifts
3. *General gifts.* Source: balance of congregation and friends

Donor Classification

All names are placed in division categories of the standard chart.

Donor Evaluation

Carefully review each name in each of the two top divisions. This evaluation process will attempt to arrange prospects into gift categories within their division. This is not assigning a subscription amount but rather making the best possible judgment of what the donor prospect might give if properly motivated. It is important to match the gift potential to the categories in the standard chart. Using the chart as the prime guide, the evaluation committee (four to six of the most knowledgeable people in the congregation who themselves are generally among the larger donors) attempts to locate at least two to three names for candidates for each category above the top line on the chart. It is imperative to focus first on the leadership gifts above the top line.

The major purpose of the evaluation process is to discover where the money is. Someone once asked an infamous bank robber why he robbed banks. He replied, "Because that's where the money is." As crass as it may sound, when raising large dollars for capital funds, you must go to the larger donor prospects first. An old story has circulated for years about someone asking a seasoned fund-raiser, "How do you raise large dollars?" He responded, "How do you catch a moose?" Obviously you go where the moose are. That's the principle of finding the large donors for a capital campaign. You bring together all the best data to identify these large donor prospects. The evaluation process also creates the best cultivation strategy and the most effective solicitation team.

The Campaign Timetable

A campaign schedule is imperative. The size of the target, the number of prospects, and the geography of the prospects will determine the length of a capital campaign. In most parish settings, a moderate campaign should last eight to twelve months. A typical timetable follows:

1. Campaign plan adopted: April
2. Campaign organization in place: April
3. Case statement prepared: April
4. Pledge instruments prepared: April
5. Photos and renderings ready: April
6. Leadership gifts division evaluation: April
7. Q & A material complete: May
8. Brochure complete: May
9. Video complete: May
10. Leadership gifts solicited: May–July
11. Major gifts evaluation: May
12. General solicitation materials prepared: May
13. Major gifts cultivation events and solicitations: June–August

14. General cultivation events and solicitations: Aug–Oct
15. Final wrap-up (all divisions): November
16. Final report: November
17. Victory celebration: November

The Case Statement

The campaign team should create a case statement, which is a written explanation of the reasons and target for the capital campaign. This document becomes the prime reference on which all the other materials (e.g., brochure, video, Q & A) are developed and the events are planned. When the case statement is completed, the team has declared its focused intentions. Everybody is "reading from the same page."

The case statement should include:

- a statement on the history and mission of the congregation;
- a listing of the needs that have come out of the vision initiative;
- a list of proposed solutions to these needs (repairs, upgrades, land acquisition, new construction, etc.);
- the financial costs to solve the problems;
- the target of the campaign; and
- the timetable for the campaign.

The case statement will usually be prepared by the professional fund-raiser (if the church uses professional counsel) or guided by the nonprofessional campaign director. This case statement may be used in the leadership gifts cultivation and solicitation contacts.

Beginning the Campaign

Phase 1: Securing the Leadership Gifts

The leadership gifts prospects are the donors who have been placed in the category for the top ten gifts needed. These prospects are carefully assigned to the team member who will make the most compelling appeal. Sometimes this is the senior pastor, since some very large donors want to "talk to the person in charge." Usually the pastor will be accompanied by another church leader, preferably one who has made a large commitment or is in a financial position to make a leadership gift. In some instances, the professional fundraising consultant may accompany the pastor or another assigned caller. I have usually done this, but sometimes the professional will not agree to make these calls.

The prospect should be told in advance that the purpose of the call is to discuss the capital campaign. Many of them have already been surveyed in the feasibility study, so they are aware of the appeal. At this first meeting, the visiting team should consider the following principles:

- Inform the prospect of the reasons for the campaign, referring to the studies and conclusions of the vision initiative.
- Highlight the case statement and perhaps leave a copy with the prospect. (It is usually not wise to have a brochure ready to distribute at this early stage of the campaign. Brochures are quickly circulated among the people and that disrupts the timing of the campaign.)
- This phase of the campaign is often referred to as the "quiet" or "select" phase. The leadership gifts

prospects should be seen personally and not in groups. Unless there are reasons to the contrary, both husband and wife should be called on together. A leadership gift represents a large commitment. The prospects should be visited in their homes or the church the first time, not in a public place such as a restaurant.

Gifts of the size sought in this campaign have several special considerations:

- Leadership gifts may be considered as designated gifts with the possibility of a room or building being named in honor of the donor or their families/ friends. Some congregations have rulings against naming anything for a donor or posting a donor's name in public. Before a name is placed on any building or other public place, it should be a significant gift. However, designated gifts or "memorials" often produce a large commitment. Do not place the name publicly on the basis of the pledge only. "Memorials" are posted when the dollars are received.

  Once I was called upon by a college who had changed its name because of a large commitment. The story hit the front page of the *Wall Street Journal*. As a result, giving from other sources dried up because the school had "so much money." The problem was that the donor didn't have the resources to match the commitment. That error was very costly. So only place a name when the funds are in, unless that gift is backed up with an irrevocable trust.

- All major commitments should have some instrument such as a codicil to the donor's will, but prefer- ably will have an irrevocable trust instrument to guarantee the donor that their wishes will be carried out even if they are not around for the fulfillment of the commitment. I never met a sincere large donor who didn't appreciate this suggestion.

- Some leadership gifts may need to be amplified with a deferred gift, i.e., a gift out of the donor's estate. This is especially attractive for older donor prospects who are not positioned to release their total gift at the time of the appeal but are positioned to assure a portion of their gift from their estate. The church may not spend these deferred gifts until the terms of the planned gift have been fulfilled. However, a properly documented promise of a deferred gift is often a valuable instrument in securing funds to help meet the needs. It is wise to show the donor prospect the standard chart but only the categories above the first line (the top ten gifts). Ask the prospect if they see themselves in this range of gifts. Let them know that the payout period may be negotiated.

- A pledge card prepared with the prospect's name and address is left with the prospect.

- In church campaigns, it is often appropriate to have prayer with the prospects. Ask the donor to contact the caller when the commitment is ready to be received. The calling team must follow up to make certain that the verbal commitment, if any, is finalized. The campaign team, especially those who have been assigned the leadership gifts donor prospects, should meet weekly for reporting and strategy.

Phase 2: Securing the Major Gifts

The major gifts are those that fall into the midrange of the standard chart (above the second line). The following guidelines apply to soliciting at this level:

- Assign major gifts prospects to a team member.
- The team member should personally invite the prospects to a small cultivation event.
- The campaign brochure and Q & A are distributed at this event.
- The campaign video is shown at this event.
- The pastor and some team members should make an appeal for support.
- Pledge cards, with each prospect's name and address in the proper space, are distributed.
- The team member who has been assigned the major gift prospect(s) will follow up to completion.

Phase 3: Securing General Gifts

The balance of the constituency is cultivated and solicited in the third phase of the campaign. Far more prospects are involved, but the dollars committed are far less. Most of the congregation thinks this general gift phase *is* the campaign. The plan is to have the leadership gifts and the major gifts committed by the time phase three begins. This announcement gives a lift to the congregation and assures them that the campaign is real and achievable. The general gift appeal will follow these guidelines:

- Include every member in the church.
- Generally a church dinner or a series of church dinners will be held to inform, cultivate, and solicit the general donors.
- This is a high-energy event. Where phase one and two are quiet, phase three is noisy. This is the time for the balloons and whistles. The program should be exciting. The speakers should be informative

134

and persuasive. Sometimes it is appropriate to have a leadership gift donor give a testimony regarding his or her involvement if the donor is a good communicator.

- The Q & A is at each table space at the beginning of the program.
- The brochure and commitment cards (along with an envelope addressed to the church) are distributed toward the end of the program.
- The donors are asked to sign their pledge cards at the dinner. A celebration of commitment is designed to receive the pledge cards.

The campaign follow-up should be accomplished through:

- pulpit reports of campaign progress
- parish newsletters
- local press publicity when appropriate (Note: Do not publicize leadership gifts too early in the campaign.)
- telephone calls
- final letters to everyone who hasn't pledged

Some large church campaigns may choose to feature a special "Million Dollar Sunday" or "Miracle Sunday." This is exciting and generates a happy giving spirit. I knew of one church that took the pledges in a wheelbarrow on "Million Dollar Sunday," symbolizing that the construction was starting with these gifts.

The important point of a "Million Dollar Sunday" is the timing. Make sure that you don't motivate a donor prospect to make a token commitment for "Million Dollar Sunday" when the standard chart may call for a

$1 million gift on top and he or she is the prime prospect for that top gift.

Time the "Million Dollar Sunday" with the opening of the general gifts solicitation phase, and use some of the gifts already committed in the reporting process if you need to publicize the success of the commitment day.

Summary

A successful capital campaign will grow out of these suggestions:

- The campaign must grow out of a "needs package."
- Large gifts must be secured first.
- Designated and deferred gifts should be considered.
- A campaign plan and timetable must be created and carefully followed.
- The campaign should be organized, exciting, and serious. Donors and campaign leadership alike must believe that "God will bring the increase."

8

STEWARDSHIP IN PERPETUITY

You may recall the old joke about two guys standing on the street corner when a funeral procession passes by. Right in the middle of the procession was a Brinks truck. One of the onlookers quipped to the other, "There goes someone who thought that they could take it with them." We laugh at this because we know that our transition out of the earthly life does not allow for space to take along anything material.

But the real truth is that we *can* "take it with us"! That is, we can make investments in those things that will keep working and producing for the kingdom after we are gone. I call this "stewardship in perpetuity." This concept is consistent with our Christian belief in eternal life. We may protect the investments we have made in this life by providing for their continuance even after we move on to our eternal life.

For example, let's assume we have been contributing funds to keep the mission of our local church alive. When we are no longer here to contribute, what will happen to the mission? It will either be cut or someone else will need to be brought in to "fill the gap." Of course we want to bring new people into our churches. That is the heart of evangelism. But think how much better it would be and how much further the church's mission could be advanced if we made provision, as we are able, for our contributions to continue after we have departed. That's really exciting—to know that our efforts will be funding the church long after we are gone. Think how important and valuable it will be for the congregation in the future.

If you are a tither in your current stewardship commitment, you may want to think of leaving at least 10 percent of your estate to the church and the other institutions you may support through your tithes and offerings.

Estate planning is an important and necessary process that everyone with any material wealth should consider. Couples often do this together. At the top of their material worth and its distribution is the concern for the other's financial welfare after either dies. That is the way it should be. Therefore a deferred stewardship gift may often be distributed after the death of the surviving spouse.

Every estate has different demands and purposes. Whenever the distribution is made, good stewardship will give serious consideration for providing income to the church after the member is gone. This is called "planned giving."

This deferred aspect of stewardship may be the most neglected and yet holds the most opportunity of any. It is especially important for church leaders to take the challenge of planned giving now. Within the next few years, an estimated trillions of dollars will pass through the estates of the current "greatest generation" to the next generation, the "baby boomers." Ironically statistics also suggest that this generation may not need the resources. In fact many boomers have more wealth than their parents. A large windfall from an estate gift, not properly designed, may even be costly to the recipient. Of course, this is not the situation for many. But that large pool of estate funds should make the church face this challenge and see the opportunity. Estate gifts may be, more than any other gift source, the future hope of meeting the dollar demands facing the church.

- Pastors should preach on stewardship in perpetuity.
- Congregations should study it.
- Church study groups should teach it.
- Church planners should promote it.
- Church leaders should practice it.
- Programs and events should be planned to cultivate estate gifts.

Estate Planning

Good stewardship gives serious consideration to planning for distribution of resources after a person has died. A *will* is the instrument that is often used in specifying what will happen to the dollars that a person has worked hard and long to create. Typically a will represents an accounting of all our material assets projected at death and how we want them handled after we are gone. If we don't provide ahead of time for a distribution of the assets, the state will. This could prove costly in tax dollars and other expenses and would probably not represent what a person intended to happen to his or her resources. You don't want to die intestate. Everybody should consider a will and keep it updated.

Most Christians with any significant assets probably have a will or an estate plan. However, studies show 90 percent of church members have not included the church as a recipient for any of their estate dollars. As congregations get older and as aging church members are showing less desire to leave their entire estates to their families, churches should be busy developing ways to attract these dollars. Most of the viable prospects for this fund-raising appeal are older with considerable assets to leave behind. Each congregation should strategize and plan for a constant appeal to attract these deferred gifts.

- The donors in this giving division should be informed of the opportunities and motivated to participate.
- The church must be busy cultivating the relationships with this donor group.
- The church must radiate trust, confidence, and credibility since this deferred gift may be the largest the donor has ever given. They want to know it will be in good hands and used wisely.

Prospecting for Deferred Gifts

A "planned giving committee" should be created to prospect, cultivate, solicit, and guide candidates who should know about and be given the opportunity to make gifts to their church through their estate. In most congregations, this committee should include:

- the pastor and staff associate where appropriate
- the church business administrator and/or church treasurer

- a person knowledgeable about the church giving records
- a person who may be knowledgeable about members' financial resources
- an attorney, particularly one professionally involved in estate planning
- a security broker, real estate broker, and insurance agent
- a financial planner

This group should meet regularly to develop the planned giving program and to guide the appeal for candidates.

Cultivating Deferred Gifts

When a list of candidates has been developed, a simple Christian estate planning event should be organized, to which each prospect is invited. The event is more successful if it is not too large. About six to ten carefully selected people (or couples) is best. It is generally advisable to assign each person to a member of the committee, who invites and encourages the prospect(s) to attend the event. It is generally wise to hold this event in a quiet and comfortable room in the church. The program should be informative, persuasive, and clear. The program should include:

- the concept of stewardship in perpetuity
- information regarding the sources for creating these planned gifts, such as securities, real estate, savings, or other investments

Methods of distributing these gifts should be presented in clear and simple form including:

1. wills
2. life insurance
3. charitable remainder trust (CRT)
4. charitable annuity trust
5. charitable annuities
6. pooled incomes
7. life estates
8. lead trust

After the presentation on sources for funding and methods for distribution is completed, provide ample opportunity for prospects to ask questions of a general nature. The attendees also should be given opportunity to invite follow-up. A simple "Yes, I'm interested" card will suffice. They should be encouraged to talk with an attorney. However, some attorneys are not receptive to the concept of recommending and assisting their clients in making these gifts. Although this concern has been raised, I have found, over the years, that most attorneys only have the best interest of their clients in focus and are generally most cooperative in carrying out their clients' wishes. The recipient institution should honor questions and requests for information from attorneys. The committee should be prepared to furnish this information and cooperate in any way to assist the donor's attorney in creating the necessary instruments. The donor's attorney should be the fund-raiser's "best friend."

Often the prospective donor does not have an attorney guiding their estate distribution. The church should have a list of attorneys, skillful in this phase of law and dedicated to the best results for the donor prospect, ready to recommend. The committee should carefully prepare the list and keep it updated. There need be no concern about conflict of interest if the donor is made aware that the recommended attorney is an independent professional and the church is not involved in any way in the fee structure. The committee, carefully formed, will thoughtfully think through all the ramifications of an attorney's involvement in the transaction.

Methods for Creating Planned Gifts

1. *A simple will* is one way in which people may transfer at death a portion of their wealth to the church. Wills may be created by the donor and even handwritten (a "holographic will"). However, it is recommended that the donor's final will be drafted by an attorney. The attorney will design the instrument of estate distribution as the donor wishes and be helpful in creating a will that may be "tax friendly" to heirs.

A will also designates an executor—the person, bank, or trust company who administrates the donor's wishes. It is important that an executor:

- be reliable and ethical
- follow the instructions of the will
- protect the interests of the beneficiaries
- respect and work within the tax laws and guidelines
- be careful and wise in investing the corpus of the will
- evaluate and respect any legal claims to the will

Often a fee is connected with the executor's services. A person may save this fee by naming a spouse or adult child as executor. However, this should be done with care, depending on the size of the will and the business acumen and reliability of the relative. An attorney can offer advice on selecting an executor.

2. *Life insurance* has often been used by people to make deferred gifts to the institution of their choice. This is especially attractive to younger donors because they are able to purchase life insurance at very attractive rates while they are young. (Sometimes, at a later age, people cannot fund gifts through life insurance because they are uninsurable because of health reasons.) All premiums for life insurance designated to a charitable cause are tax deductible. It is often wise to consider making the church the owner of the policy. This may quiet any beneficiary claims. This affords the donor the security that these gift dollars will be allocated as the donor desired.

3. *A charitable remainder trust (CRT)* is a highly desirable instrument to make a deferred gift to the church.

- It can be designed so that it cannot be changed. This protects the donor's intention.
- The donor may designate how the gift will be used.
- The donor avoids paying capital gains tax on whatever is put into the trusts, e.g., stocks, bonds, real estate, or other gifts in kind. This is an extremely attractive tax savings.
- The donor may receive a tax deduction for the gift.
- The donor may receive an income from the trust. The income may be spread over the life of the donor and spouse. When it moves down into more beneficiaries, it reduces much of the tax incentives and dramatically reduces the income benefit.
- The remainder of the trust, after the lifetime of the donor(s), goes to the church. This will guarantee stewardship in perpetuity, allowing the donor to offer a lasting and ongoing gift.

4. *A charitable remainder annuity trust* is much the same as a CRT. It differs largely in the way the income from the trust is distributed. The CRT is a percentage payment against the earnings in the trusts, while the annuity specifies a fixed amount to be paid each year.

5. *A charitable annuity* is usually a commercial annuity that is transferred to the church as a gift. It has large tax incentives and is sometimes used as a gift to the church.

6. *Pooled income* is a pool of gifts under one management. A local congregation, a group of congregations, a denomination, or an association may create such a fund. The gifts from several donors are put into the same fund. This larger aggregation of funds may offer investment incentives and advantages. Many of the same conditions of the CRT apply. It may be particularly valuable for some congregations to create the pooled fund. A bank is often an important ally in establishing and managing such a fund. Like the other methods for distribution of gifts, issues such as income to the donor and tax consequences of the pooled income fund should be discussed with a consulting attorney.

7. *A life estate* often has its source in real estate. I have seen this type of gifting used on several occasions. A donor deeds over their property and is allowed the right to continue to live in the residence for the rest of their lifetime. At the time of deeding over the property, the donor benefits from a tax deduction. Upon the death of the donor, the property passes over to the church, which usually sells it for proceeds to use in its mission. This transaction takes the property out of the donor's estate. Therefore it does not go through probate and avoids estate taxes.

8. *A lead trust* is basically the opposite of a remainder trust. Through this instrument, funds are passed along

to the congregation for a fixed period of time. During that time the church uses the income. At the end of the time, the corpus passes back to the original donor's estate with tax savings benefit. This instrument takes the earnings out of the donor's tax responsibility and provides an attractive tax incentive for the donor as a charitable gift. This may have a very attractive appeal to someone whose heirs will not need the money until a later date. The donor can make a gift to the church and fulfill his stewardship desire, receive tax benefits, and still provide for his heirs as planned. This complex instrument should have the guidance of the donor's attorney and tax advisor. The church should make information about lead trusts available to the congregation. Some may find it appealing.

Related to planned giving are additional areas that the church planned giving committee should be familiar with in order to best serve the donor.

- *Living trusts.* People of more than average wealth may consider the creation of a living trust. There are distinct tax advantages in creating this trust. It is the best assurance a person has that money is in place for his or her long-term care and arrangement, both mentally and physically. It gives firm direction for distributing final assets to family, friends, and charities. One of the attractive features of a living trust is that the donor still controls his or her resources but has placed the dollars in a trust position when final directions will be honored and the estate will enjoy the tax benefits. An attorney is needed to prepare a living trust. If a person's net worth is large enough, a living trust should be considered. The trust directs

146

the donor's intentions of fulfilling stewardship in perpetuity.

- *Living will.* This instrument directs family and all health care providers as to what medical procedures a person will want and not want if he or she becomes terminally ill and cannot give directions. Sometimes the document may say that if the patient's condition is hopeless, from the professional medical point of view, no life-prolonging measures will be used. Comfort and dignity in dying is at the direction of the patient. This subject is becoming more significant and should be part of the understanding of the patient's minister.

Powers of Attorney and Conservatorship

These are legal documents that allow another person to act on someone's behalf.

- *Power of attorney.* Broad powers are given to a person (attorney or not) to handle financial matters. These powers are revoked when a person is mentally incapacitated and may need this service the most.
- *Durable power of attorney.* This gives the selected person the power to act on another's behalf even if that person on whose behalf they are acting is mentally incapacitated.
- *Conservatorship.* A conservator is often appointed to handle someone's affairs if that person is unable. Often this conservator is appointed by the state and may not be someone a person would select. Some states may honor a nomination for conservator, but

this will not be necessary if someone has been granted durable power of attorney.

More about the Charitable Remainder Trust (CRT)

The most used of all the instruments for creating deferred gifts is the charitable remainder trust. Douglas K. Freeman, senior partner of Freeman, Freeman, and Smiley, L.L.O. with offices in Los Angeles and Irvine, California, is considered by many the most knowledgeable expert on CRTs in America. For thirty years he has provided wise counsel to individuals regarding planned-giving arrangements. He also consults with many of the largest nonprofit institutions on methods for developing and operating charitable remainder trusts as a key factor in their fund-raising programs. Through the years I have been privileged to work with him in this institutional capacity, and I thank him for his wise counsel. He is the best! He has published a guidebook on charitable remainder trusts, including the most asked questions, and has granted me permission to use some of this informative material. I thank him for this information.

Question: What is a "Charitable Remainder Trust" (CRT)?

Answer: A Charitable Remainder Trust or "CRT" is a trust that is created to provide a distribution of income to an individual or other non-charitable entity for a period of time, with the balance or "remainder interest" passing to a charity at the termination of a trust.

Question: Why should I consider a CRT?

Answer: These trusts provide important tax, economic and philanthropic benefits to the creator or "donors."

A contribution to a CRT will entitle the donor to receive a current income tax deduction, based on the present value of the gift that will ultimately pass to the charity. The tax deduction can be applied against all forms of income (salary, interest, dividends, and capital gains), thereby reducing the personal taxes the donor would otherwise have paid. Assets owned by a CRT can be sold by the trust without tax either to the trust or to the donor. Avoiding capital gains tax is an important benefit.

The donor, or other income beneficiary, will be entitled to distributions from the trust until the trust terminates (either at the death of the income beneficiary or after a specific number of years).

The assets in this trust will ultimately pass to charity, thereby reducing the donor's estate and any taxes due on the death of the donor. Following the termination of the trust, the remaining assets will pass to one or more charities selected by the donor thereby making a major gift for philanthropy.

Question: What types of Charitable Remainder Trust can be created?

Answer: There are two broad categories of Charitable Remainder Trust. The first category is known as a Charitable Remainder "Annuity" Trust. This type of instrument provides that the income recipient will receive a fixed dollar income amount each year and the trust based on a percentage of the original value of the trust assets. Regardless of what happens to the value of the trust, the income recipient is guaranteed a flat payment each year. That flat payment is called an annuity.

The second type of trust is known as the *"unitrust."* It pays the income recipient a fixed percentage of the annual fair market value of the trust assets. In effect this is a variable annuity, since the payment can go up (if the value of the trust grows) or down (if the value of the trust declines). The percentage remains the same, but, since the value of the principle can change the amount of the distribution can change.

Question: Which is the best trust for me?
Answer: The answer to this question depends upon your particular circumstances, including your income needs and the liquidity of the trust itself.

Question: Who can I designate as the income bene-ficiaries?
Answer: You may appoint yourself or anyone else you want. You should always consult your tax advisor before designating anyone other than yourself or your spouse. It is often said that CRT is a "win/win" instrument. The recipient organization "wins" when it gets the remainder of the funds at the termination of the trust, and the donor "wins" with guaranteed income, income tax deductions, and the dollars are taken out of the estate so there is no estate tax on them.[1]

This information from Doug Freeman will be very helpful to you in the strategy.

I have had the privilege of seeing many of these CRTs developed. Here is a classic example of a CRT from my experience of consulting with a large Presbyterian retirement home in planned giving.

- A woman lived in a church retirement home. She was widowed and in her late eighties.
- Her husband was a wise investor. He had put money into growth stocks before he died. These stocks showed enormous gains but paid little or no income.
- Due to inflation, the value of the dollar had eroded and the woman was having cash-flow difficulties.

150

- If she had sold her securities and purchased bonds or other income-producing commodities, she would have faced enormous capital gains taxes.
- She had no children but she had a nephew she wanted to "remember with something."
- Her assets were transferred to a nonprofit religious group of her choice. The institution sold the assets, but neither she nor the institution paid any capital gains tax.
- She was paid income more than three times what she had been "trying to live on" before.
- Because of her age, she received a generous income tax deduction which she spread over six years. This offset any taxes she would pay on her income from the trust.
- When the stocks were sold, a fully paid-up life insurance policy on her life was purchased, with her nephew designated as the beneficiary. This is often referred to as wealth replacement.
- She felt secure. She had ample money for her daily needs. Her estate faced no taxes.
- She was a philanthropist. Her husband's name and hers were placed as a memorial in a room because of the size of her gift.

This was truly a "win-win" situation.

Giving through a Foundation

An eleemosynary foundation is an entity established for a charitable cause. It comes from the Greek word *eleemosyne* and means "to take pity." In the New Testament, it was the word used for distributing alms. The root of the word is *eeloor,* which means "mercy." Jesus talked about the Pharisees who were obsessed with the legal aspect of tithing but neglected mercy (Luke 11:41–42). In another passage he said, "Do not lay up for yourselves treasures on earth, where moth and rust destroy and where thieves break in and steal; but lay up for yourselves treasures in heaven, where neither moth nor rust destroys and where thieves do not break in and steal. For where your treasure is, there your heart will be also" (Matt. 6:19–21). In the Old Testament, God's proclamation to Israel reaches a zenith when the prophet says:

> He has shown you, O man, what is good; and what does the LORD require of you but to do justly, to love mercy, and to walk humbly with your God?
>
> Micah 6:8

This may well be called Rules and Guides for Living.

A charitable foundation is an instrument created to do mercy, distribute alms, and lift the quality of life for others. A foundation is often established by an individual, a group of people, a family, a corporation, or any organization that desires to have a part of its action focused on charity.

In essence, a foundation is generally a "not-for-profit organization" that comes under section 501(c)(3) of the Internal Revenue Code. As such it may receive gifts that are tax free to the donor and are distributed to individual philanthropies. Foundation giving represents the largest percentage of charitable gifts outside individual gifts.

Foundations have many attractive features as an arm for giving. They are generally used for the distribution of larger amounts of money. They are relevant to church giving because they may offer a significant source of gifts for certain causes of the congregation. Some larger churches are establishing a foundation "part of but separate from" the congregation. This separate entity may become attractive to some donors and may be a valuable means for acquiring and distributing designated funds to causes outside the budget of the church. Little, if any, tax advantage may exist for a church to establish a foundation "to run alongside the congregation corporation" since they are both 501(c)(3). However, the value of a foundation as an appeal for gifts beyond the congregation and the value of handling certain funds outside the routine direction of the congregation may make a foundation worthwhile.

Fixed guidelines are set up for establishing and managing a foundation. A competent attorney acquainted with this field of law is important for any person, family, group, corporation, or church desiring to "distribute its alms" in this organized fashion. It is an important subject in the whole field of church fund-raising.

Summary

These various methods of accepting and distributing charitable gifts, whether current or deferred, are like the instruments in a great symphony orchestra. Each is important and should be given the individual attention the instrumentalist gives to his or her part in making the production a success. Each church should be constantly sharpening all its fund-raising materials.

9

CREATING AND MANAGING ENDOWMENT FUNDS

Every church should consider establishing an endowment fund. To endow means, "to give money or property so as to provide income for support of a college, church, hospital, or other charitable organization." The key word is *income*. The dollars working in the endowment fund are often different "use dollars" than dollars in an operating or capital fund. In an endowment fund, the corpus, i.e., the main substance of the fund, generally remains untouched, and that amount is usually invested. The income from the corpus, generally calculated and distributed annually or by special call, affords the church a stream of income beyond the regular gifts.

Many churches do not have endowment funds because they make no effort to create plans for receiving them, a system for managing them, and a method for distributing the income. Meeting the challenges of each of these points becomes the starting place for every congregation that seriously wants to have this additional stream of income.

Sometimes money is left in a legacy to the church at the time of the death of a member. Often the church board is not aware of the gift provision and really does not know what to do about proceeds from the gift. If the church has an endowment in place, these gifts, unless otherwise specified, have a positive parking place for the future needs of the congregation.

As in the case of deferred gifts, an endowment committee should be established. This committee generally should include:

- the pastor
- selected staff person(s), where advisable
- the church treasurer
- several members-at-large who have knowledge of investments and trust management

The purpose of the committee will be:

- to study endowments and how they work;
- to determine how the fund will be invested and managed;
- to set the boundaries for protection of the fund and create the endowment fund policies;
- to provide a system of reporting;
- to inform the congregation of the existence of the endowment fund; and
- to aggressively reach out to generate dollars for the fund.

The appeals for developing an endowment fund are similar to developing dollars for operating the church or capital dollars to upgrade or expand the church. They are driven by the principle of stewardship.

However, churches do not stress endowment funds as much as operating funds and capital funds because they are generally related to future income. Yet every congregation should be thinking of its future and sources of income to supplement the current needs. An endowment fund is generally the best means of securing and managing these funds.

Establishing a single endowment fund is the starting place for most congregations. All the policies for creating, managing, and distributing the fund will be the initial concern of the committee. The endowment fund may have several causes as its initial distribution focus. Within a single endowment fund may be subendowment purposes, but the primary fund is under a single rubric. Larger congregations may create and manage several funds separately. However, they should all be under the oversight of the endowment committee.

Purposes of the Endowment Fund

Several purposes exist for the church's established income distribution goals. They are:

General Church Funds

As dollars spin off from the fund's investments, they are placed into the church's regular operating account and may be used by the church leadership for any purpose most needed. Thus they are often referred to as "unrestricted funds." Where there is an established endowment, budget planners may use these unrestricted dollars in projecting the income to help offset budget needs. This is usually determined by projected income from earnings of the endowment fund.

Needs and conditions within a church change from time to time, so it is not wise to have all endowment income restricted for particular purposes. In fact, the policies of the fund should allow for restricted dollars to move into the general purpose or another designated purpose, should the restricted cause no longer exist. Studies show that many gifts have been made for specific causes, yet the need for such no longer exists. Those funds are lying idle in the banks instead of actively funding the work of the church. This is not good stewardship.

Occasionally a church may be asked to allow an outside cause to come under its endowment fund because the cause does not have nonprofit status. This should be studied very carefully; it is usually best to resist the offer. Everything related to the endowment fund has certain legal and IRS guidelines. The church must be meticulous in the way it establishes, manages, and distributes endowment funds. Integrity, responsibility, and accountability are crucial.

Endowment funds often keep a church alive. Some of our great old congregations would have closed their doors if not for income from endowments to service their programs and maintain buildings and grounds. As the demographics in a community change, church attendance and support often change too. The income from the current congregation cannot pay the bills. If an endowment has been in place, the earned dollars serve as mission dollars for the church's own parish, providing a base for a new congregation, brought about by demographic changes, to develop its own support system.

Sometimes unrestricted endowment funds may work a hardship on the congregation. Instead of using the endowment dollars to provide outreach programs and relevant promotion to the "new" community surrounding the church, the dollars accrued are used excessively to service dying programs. The congregation chooses not to reach out to the newer community. Attendance and programs drop off. No effort is really made to bring in current congregational dollars to support the programs. The church begins to live off of the endowment, and the congregation begins to die. To prevent this, the church should establish policies, in the early days of establishing an endowment, or at least before a demographic shift, that those endowment earnings may not be used to support programs. However, they may be used for:

- maintaining the buildings and grounds
- maintaining the staff for basic leadership needs
- engaging new staff, especially trained and gifted, to promote the church within the new community

In establishing an endowment policy and looking to the future, some churches have set a ceiling on the amount of a general endowment that may be used to meet the annual budget. This ceiling has sometimes been 50 percent, where income from the endowment will not exceed half of the annual expenses. Income over that percentage may be distributed to missions, local and otherwise.

These endowment policy restrictions may help overcome later congregational lethargy. Dollars put into a church's endowment fund are valuable for the long term. One church I know would not have been able to make significant gifts to its community and other worthwhile missions had it not been for the generous endowment fund created by many donors over many years. Clear-cut policies and responsible management are important.

Of course, any limiting policies may apply only to the unrestricted endowment dollars for distribution and not the restricted funds. These are treated differently.

Mission Causes

Monies collected for specific mission causes, or for missions in general, are usually restricted funds for allocation. Bequests to the church may often carry these restrictions. The restrictions should be respected and carried out as the donor requested. If the church does not wish to support the limiting proposed uses, the committee should try to negotiate alternative designations or be prepared to refuse the gift. This will seldom happen.

Mission dollars are frequently an attractive purpose for developing endowment funds. Whenever these funds are established, the church should keep the congregation, especially the donors to the designated endowment, informed about the service and status of the mission cause. If for any reason the mission ceases to exist, the church should have an alternative use for the income—a "like" cause. It is wise, whenever possible, for the terms of distribution to have a provision to accomplish this.

Educational Causes

The same guidelines for designated endowment dollars to mission causes apply to educational causes.

A congregation may select, or a donor may request, that the income from a specific endowment be distributed to a certain educational institution. If this is the case, the institution should keep the church informed on the status of the institution and how these gift dollars have been distributed. If the corpus came from a single donor, or a family, the church should make every effort to keep the specific donor informed.

A scholarship fund may be selected by a congregation, or a donor through the congregation, for a specific institution. The scholarships often carry the name of the individual donor, the name of the church, or the name of someone that the church wishes to honor. These endowment funds are often attractive to groups within the congregation. The women's association of a church I once served as pastor established a scholarship in my name at a seminary. Throughout the years, dollars have been added, and the spin-off has helped a number of students meet the financial demands of higher education. The fact that a fund was established and designated for a specific purpose encouraged interest and support long after the initial gift.

Some churches will create an endowment fund for scholarships for higher education of their own young people. These funds are often very appealing to donors because of their involvement with the recipients. Not only does the gift help fund the educational experience of the student; it often binds the relationship of the student to the church for a lifetime.

Scholarship endowment funds are appealing because people may put money into the fund of any amount, at any time, and know that it will actively be distributed under the terms of the fund.

Maintenance and Repair Causes

Perhaps the most difficult endowment dollar to generate is that of providing funds to maintain the buildings and grounds. To many donors it may not seem as exciting as giving to people projects such as missionaries, educators, and students. And yet it may be the most important use of endowment funds. A well-constructed church that is kept clean, attractive, and in good repair (where the landscape is maintained, the musical instruments are in tune, the signs and bulletin boards are attractive, and the walls are pleasantly decorated; where the hymnbooks, Bibles, and other worship items are in good repair; where the sound system is good, the climate is comfortable, the rest rooms are clean and comfortable, and people get a general feeling of tidiness and order) will be a church that people want to attend. Maintenance and attention takes money. If these dollars come out of endowment funds rather than operational funds, the budget dollars saved can be used for needed program costs. People who make capital gifts for buildings and grounds expect to see them maintained. These same people may be persuaded to protect the capital investment by making maintenance dollars available through an endowment fund, knowing that these dollars will keep on working and the property will be maintained long after they have gone.

More people are giving to endowments designated for the practical reason of keeping the buildings and grounds in good repair than ever before. Although the dollars are restricted to buildings and grounds, the church leadership may use these dollars where most needed within this broad operational area and release other dollars for program costs. I would place the endowment for maintenance as a high priority in appeal.

Managing the Endowment Fund

Each local congregation must decide carefully how the endowment will be managed.

- Who will manage and guide the investments made by the fund to produce the surest and best income?
- Who will be responsible to see that the terms of the trust are carefully carried out?
- Who will direct the distribution of the funds so that the causes for which the money was designated receive their appropriate share?
- Who will keep a record of all financial transactions for the fund, including gifts given, investments, and distribution?
- Who will prepare the accurate accounting so that all concerned are informed and the legal requirements have all been met?

These questions, and others that will arise, must be carefully studied and answered properly so that everyone will be confident with the integrity of the trust. The endowment may be administered by the officers of the church, a special board of elected trustees, or an outside administrator such as a bank or a trust company. Sometimes the administration is carried out jointly through internal and external administration. Some denominations have a foundation to assist local congregations in management and distribution of endowment dollars. All options and alternatives should be carefully studied, in concert with legal counsel and trust experts. Setting up the guidelines properly is critical for establishing and managing an endowment fund. Having created the endowment instrument, it then becomes critical to create the resources for establishing the fund.

Sources of Funds for the Endowment

Money sometimes comes into the church for endowment purposes when the church doesn't have an endowment or know how to handle one. Think what could happen if the church aggressively sought to create endowment dollars with the same intensity that it raises operating and capital dollars. Let's look at some possible sources for developing endowment funds.

Estates

Bequests were considered in chapter 8 on deferred gifts. Those gifts are not always related to an endowment. However, many times donors may wish a portion or all of their estate to go into an endowment, designated or undesignated. These gifts have long-range value and should be encouraged. The terms of the endowment should be clearly defined. If the purpose of the endowment is specified but may not have long-range protection, after naming the specific purpose, the conditions may include: "or for such other purposes as the official board may from time to time determine." With this provision the wishes of the donor may be respected as long as the need exists, but the church is free to use the money for other objectives when the circumstances change. Like all bequests, it is wise for the church to have legal guidance in establishing specific endowments.

Memorials

Sometimes a person dies and the family and friends wish to remember that person with gifts to an endowment. If a church endowment fund already exists, the money goes into the existing fund but bears the name of the person being memorialized as a special category in the fund. A named gift to the endowment fund may be given to honor a pastor, a spouse, or any person someone wishes to name. Each time such an endowment gift is received, it should go into the general endowment, even though it may be designated for missions, education, maintenance, etc. A separate endowment separately managed should only occur when the gift is of a major dollar amount.

An existing endowment, where people may make contributions in memory or in honor of someone, is a very attractive gift instrument. This fund should always be open to receive general gifts when a family requests a contribution to the endowment fund in lieu of flowers.

Sometimes a family may create a named endowment within the church's endowment trust. The family may wish to have some say regarding the distribution and allow the trustees of the endowment to administrate.

Recognition Gifts

Money for the endowment fund may be generated by offering donors a name recognition appeal: for example, an official endowment record. This may be a permanent book on display, carefully prepared so that all memorials are listed clearly. It may be a "wall of memory" on which the names of people honored or memorialized are permanently displayed, either inside or outside the church building. Space should be provided for the wall to be added onto through the generations.

Walk of Faith

Robert Schuller at the Crystal Cathedral established attractive stepping-stones around the campus. Each granite stone has a Scripture verse and the name of the donor. Our verse reads: "The Lord is my light and my salvation; Whom shall I fear?" (Ps. 27:1). As people walk around the campus, they stop and read the uplifting Scriptures and see the names of the people who donated for the stones. The donor makes a fixed contribution for the stone. A portion of the money goes for preparing and permanently placing the stone. The balance of the gift may be used as a permanent source of income through an endowment established for this purpose. Several other churches have taken this idea, modified it for their own situation, and developed an inspiring walk, the proceeds from which are placed in the endowment fund.

Cemetery

In the earlier days of our country, the church graveyard became the common burial site for deceased members of the church family. These parish cemeteries can still be found in much of older America. As large cities developed, commercial cemeteries gradually replaced these church cemeteries, particularly among Protestant church families. Roman Catholic churches often continued to develop and manage their own cemeteries. Lately this trend has changed, and many Protestant congregations are again establishing a memorial center on their own church campuses.

Not only does the memorial garden on the church campus offer comfort and an easier access for the family, it may become a great source of income to the church. The size and complexity of the development of a cemetery depends on the size of the congregation, the community it serves, other established cemeteries in close proximity, and the amount of land or space the church may devote for this use.

There are three methods for interment:

166

1. Ground burial
2. Wall entombment, often called a mausoleum
3. Cremation, where the body is burned and the remaining ashes are placed in an urn, scattered, or put into a niche in the wall of a columbarium

Cremation, particularly in the western United States, is becoming a more desired choice for the disposition of the human body. Many churches are developing attractive columbariums for church family use to house the cremated remains of a loved one or friend. A columbarium is a wall thick enough to enclose the metal box for the cremated remains. I have worked with some churches where this wall is in a garden, usually near the sanctuary of the church. Others have created an attractive room or alcove inside the church building, generally near the sanctuary. Columbariums are fitting in the church area and desirable for family use. They do not take much space, are reasonably simple (under proper direction) to create, and generate attractive income that a church may use for its endowment fund. For example, a U-shaped wall, twenty feet on three sides and eight feet high, with a garden in the center, will accommodate enough niches to generate nearly $1 million. At 7 percent return, that would represent seventy thousand dollars in annual return. This is a marvelous source for endowment dollars.

Some churches create a memorial park that provides for interment in all three standard forms. This requires ground space for casket burial, wall space for casket entombment, and wall and ground space for cremation containers. This full-service cemetery takes more space and costs more money to develop but delivers more dollars in return. It is attractive because it gives families more options for memorializing loved ones in their own church.

I had the privilege of helping in the development of the memorial gardens at the Crystal Cathedral in Garden Grove, California. Although my staff position made me responsible for raising funds, the development of this beautiful memorial gardens was a natural extension of my basic job.

We received a permit from the city to create a cemetery with ten thousand interment spaces. They approved the plan, which called for approximately five thousand niches for cremated remains, twenty-five hundred crypts in the ground at a depth of two per space, and twenty-five hundred wall crypts for caskets. We included several inside enclosed family rooms and outside enclosed private family gardens. All of this was accomplished on one and one-third acres.

Now a few words of advice:

- Don't try to build too much at the start. Design a memorial property that can be enlarged as the need occurs.
- Don't overprice your inventory. Make it possible for your church family to afford it.
- Provide for a system where the purchaser may buy over time.
- Get good counsel up front, not only for design but also for engineering, permits, marketing, and management.
- Add 10 percent to each sale for perpetual care and maintenance. This maintenance need should not become a burden later for the church. The money from this additional 10 percent should be placed in a separate endowment category with the assurance that its income will only be used for care and maintenance of the cemetery.

Senior Housing

Of all the sources for generating a flow of income, as well as performing a great ministry, creating a senior housing facility may be best for larger churches with space for this purpose and a clientele large enough to make it marketable. Congregate senior housing is at the cutting edge of the future. The elderly population is skyrocketing; people are receiving better health care and living longer. Added to this normal aging trend, baby boomers will soon be joining this retirement group. It will represent the largest generation ever of senior adults.

In 2000 the United States had thirty-five million persons age sixty-five or older. By 2040, that number will increase to nearly eighty million, and that figure doesn't allow for longevity due to better health.

Many of this retirement group will seek congregate living, where they no longer need to maintain buildings and grounds or pay real-estate taxes and household insurance, and they can enjoy the peace of mind of a group setting with constant security, meals, housecleaning, and medical assistance. Experts project this to be the housing trend for the elderly in the future.

The church has an important role to play in the care for the elderly. It is a vital ministry. Senior facilities with graded forms of care are constantly being developed. For many seniors they offer clean and comfortable facilities, a good social environment, excellent food services, certain health care, and secure and safe conditions. However, there is one group of retirees, significant in size, that would desire one additional feature—an active spiritual and church environment.

For people in this group, the church has been at the center of their lives. They attended worship regularly, participated in fellowship and study groups, taught Sunday school, sang in the choir, served on boards, and raised their kids in the church. Suddenly their lives are changing. If the church could create retirement facilities on or near the church campus, these people would be happy and prospective residents.

Not only would these seniors have all the benefits of any well-managed congregate living, but they could attend church activities, serve as volunteers in many capacities, enjoy a cross-generational setting where they might be role models and mentors to children and young people, and be at home in the community they know and love the most—the church.

Churches may take several different approaches to creating senior housing on their campus.

1. *The church builds a purely independent living facility.* It rents out the apartments or villas. Part of the rental money services the loan for creating the facilities. When the loan is paid off, the net rent money may be put into an endowment fund for the church.
2. *The church builds a facility for independent living with assisted living services and meal services.* The same principle of paying off the loan with rental money applies.
3. *Individuals buy a life interest in their unit.* They will never be asked to leave. Many of these facilities will offer regular meal service, assisted living services, and in some instances, a third level of care called "skilled nursing." The financial package is clear.
4. *The prospective resident pays an accommodation fee up front.* This is a capital investment, and in many cases, all or part of this down payment comes from the sale of his or her residence. Part, all, or none of this down payment is returned to

170

the residents if they move, or to the estate at death. The sponsoring group makes that decision before marketing begins. The down payment and monthly fees are affected by the return of capital method that is used. I tend to favor a plan where the residents or their estates get a 50 to 70 percent return. However, studies and conditions will determine this decision.

5. *Residents also pay a monthly fee* for their share of the utilities, food services, social services, house-cleaning, and other services offered.

The management fee is determined by occupancy. It is wise for the church to use outside management. Residential monthly fees will cover this expense.

The church brings the land to the project. Hopefully it is on the church campus, contiguous, or near. A price for the value of the land is set before the project begins. This figure helps determine the total cost, what each unit will cost, and the resident's down payment and monthly fees. When the facility is filled, the church receives a "land draw," the valued amount of the property, but still owns and controls the project.

The usual time of occupancy for each resident, called a "generation," is about seven years. Many people are now moving into these facilities in their late seventies and eighties although the specifications are usually for persons sixty-five and older. Some live longer than others. On average, after about seven years the unit goes on the market again and the resident's estate receives the predetermined returned percentage.

The difference goes into reducing the mortgage. The monthly fee of the new owner continues to provide the services that were offered to the first owner.

By the time the second generation vacates and the unit sells, the project is paid off. After returning the agreed amount to the resident's estate, the church keeps the balance and the portion of the monthly fee that had gone to the mortgage. These dollars may well be designated to the church endowment fund.

This plan is a wonderful opportunity for both the resident and the church. If residents are so inclined, they will attend the services and support the church with their tithes and offerings; they may, if encouraged, leave part of their estate to the church.

The church is motivated to provide a ministry to senior people. It does. The church, in turn, having no investment because they get their land cost back, receives multiple financial rewards.

This is a classic example of stewardship and its rewards. It is a fantastic way to create an endowment fund.

Senior housing facilities owned by congregations are a rather new and exciting method of developing large funds for the church. I will be happy to answer further questions you might have on this subject.

EPILOGUE

Dr. Robert H. Schuller, senior pastor of the Crystal Cathedral in Garden Grove, California, and speaker/host of the long-running international television program *Hour of Power,* has created many oft-quoted sayings. One of these is: "No one has a money problem, only an *idea* problem." I would like to take my former boss's truism one step further and suggest that the *idea* itself is not completed until implemented.

This book is full of ideas and suggestions on how to raise money. The systems have proven reliable. But to actually raise the money, the ideas and systems must be implemented. The banker will not take your idea of how to raise money as collateral for loan funds to erect a new building. But he will take the money that your implemented idea has produced.

Actualize the principles in this book by overlaying your needs on the specific area of your situation. For example, if your pressing need is to raise capital dollars to build, then study that chapter carefully. Write down the points of action that appear to be workable for you and set out to implement your plan step-by-step. Set a time line to get you started and to keep you on schedule. With all of this in place, go for it!

This book is more than an outlined plan or diagram of systems to follow. Some watersheds give reason and credibility to the systems. Apply the gestalt test to reading and understanding this book. Gestalt psychology is the German school based on the idea that the response of an individual in a given situation is a response to the whole situation, not to its components. The whole context of this book can be reviewed in these highpoints:

- *Giving* is theologically sound.
- *Stewardship* is the guiding principle for our giving. Don't buy into the critics' response that stewardship is "a kind of ecclesiastical usury—a kind of sanctified extortion." The Christian concept of stewardship, that we are spiritually responsible for what God has given to us, is the breath and life for fund-raising in the church. We need a renewed emphasis, from our pulpits and church classrooms, on this biblical and time-honored principle.
- *Tithing.* Giving 10 percent of your income to support the work of the Lord is a reliable gauge for stewardship. Every congregation should stress tithing.
- *Needs.* The needs (program, capital, and mission) of a congregation should be studied constantly. They should be classified, strategized, and attractively presented to the congregation on some regular basis. Keep the people informed!
- *The process for raising funds is:*
  1. creating prospective candidates who can give
  2. informing the prospects
  3. cultivating the prospects

4. involving the prospects
5. soliciting the prospects
6. receiving commitments from the prospects
7. acknowledging the gift and following up with collection procedures

This process is the same whether the appeal is for annual support dollars or capital funds.

- *Gifts in perpetuity.* The church should constantly encourage its members to leave funds in their estates for the Lord's work.

These are the overview concepts of the book. *Study them, embrace them, implement them.* Through these principles your church will raise funds.

Now, here are some very practical observations and advice.

Seven Mistakes to Avoid

1. *Thinking too small.* Be serious about envisioning. Create the ideas to make it happen. Don't become boxed in by WNDITWB ("we never did it that way before"). Think big and outside the box. When it comes time to raise dollars, be realistic. Remember: "Rome wasn't built in a day."
2. *Not adequately preparing the congregation.* Take time and thought in doing this. It's a major mistake not to prepare the people.
3. *Not clearly developing the needs package and making the solutions winsome.*
4. *Not properly classifying and evaluating the prospects.*
5. *Not creating a challenging and workable gifts-needed chart (standards chart).* This chart will give the direction and be the driving force to make a fund-

raising campaign successful. It is like a road map. It will take you where the money is and give you a timely reference for progress. Neglecting this is a major mistake.

6. *Not following a time line.* This may be the most common mistake of all. Your plan will never happen unless you start. It will never succeed if you don't stay on schedule.

7. *Not asking.* Many times a fund-raising appeal fails because the significant prospects were not asked to give. When they do give, their gift must be acknowledged with gratitude. Making the mistake of not saying "thank you" may hinder any further appeals.

Seven Ways to Score

1. Have a bona fide needs package.
2. Have a congregation united in meeting the needs.
3. Set challenging and attainable goals.
4. Select good leadership.
5. Identify money sources and go where the money is. Get your large gifts first.
6. Design first-class informational materials.
7. Create a campaign plan. Work your plan in a timely order. Allow time to inform, cultivate, and solicit all the prospects.

Avoid Trouble Spots

Once the congregation has launched a fund-raising appeal, problem areas will arise.

A trouble-shooting catalog is needed. Sometimes the problems are personality centered. Hopefully those problems will be considered before an appeal is launched. If the campaign is underway and someone appears to be sabotaging the appeal, that person or persons should no longer be considered a part of the appeal. Preserve the integrity of the campaign even if the saboteur is lost. This will seldom happen if the congregation has done a good job in preparing for the appeal. Here are some potential trouble areas:

1. *Timing.* If the appeal is obviously not succeeding, a moratorium may need to be considered. Sometimes you will need to "go back to the drawing board." It may be that the needs package is not persuasive enough or the money just isn't there. This is one good reason why the time devoted to large gift prospects is scheduled before the general church appeal. The major amount of the money will come from this "silent" phase of the campaign. If this phase is not working, it may be time to halt the appeal or lower the dollar target.

2. *The campaign plan is wrong.* Beginning the appeal with general fund-raising events instead of focusing on the large gifts will often create a problem. People have worn themselves out and used too much time on sponsoring and running events that really don't make much money. If you find yourself in this position, it may be a time for a "graceful rest." Regroup and conduct the appeal in the time-tested order.

3. *Divided congregation.* Sometimes a fund-raising appeal will cause serious division within a church. However, if a proper feasibility study has been made before the appeal begins, this will usually not occur. If signs of division do occur, take time to consider the needs package, the size of the dollar appeal, and the realistic dollars available. Sometimes a congregation will "overgoal" or not

have the real needs some had thought. These signs require quick and definite action.

4. *Inadequate leadership.* Sometimes leadership is selected and willing to serve but does not measure up to the requirements as the appeal progresses. Or the leadership may not prove capable or willing to set the giving standards necessary to lead a campaign. That leadership must be quietly replaced.

5. *No gripping appeal.* If this happens, back off and look at the case statement, printed materials, and video. Make changes if necessary. It hasn't happened often, but I have seen campaigns pull back the brochure and create a new one if the message was not communicated effectively. Of course this should only happen if there is a large-scale negative reaction to the information materials.

6. *Inadequate systems in place.* Sometimes an appeal is begun and not enough prospect data exists to move forward with a classification, evaluation, and solicitation of donor prospects. If this becomes obvious, stop and correct the system. Adequate data is primary.

I have included these possible trouble spots in order to raise awareness in campaign leadership. Examine each of these trouble areas before going into "campaign depression." Solve them as they appear. Most of these problems will not occur if preparation is adequate. The secret is taking time to plan the appeal carefully before launching it.

Beware of Scams

Anyone who has spent much time in fund-raising is aware of unethical suggestions that come along: shady prospects, get-rich-quick ideas, fees for information, or services with an agenda other than your own.

In everything connected with your fund-raising effort, take time to examine the credentials of the source offering you services. If it is a quid pro quo offer, where you buy or do something to get a gift in return, move ahead slowly and beware. Sales and commercial organizations will make offers to the church as fund-raisers that are of little value to the people. Such offers take a lot of time and produce little result and are generally not of value.

In receiving a contribution, strings may be attached that are not worth the congregation's accepting the gift. Other than a designated gift request or a named memorial, be careful in any contributions with contingencies or conditions. Care must be taken to guard against potential "con artists." These often turn up in connection with a donor prospect. If you have reason to be suspicious, check it out. Your hunch is probably right. Not only are pyramid schemes illegal, but they can bring embarrassment and serious harm to a congregation. Stay away from them!

The Role of Leadership

You cannot expect a church to embrace the principles of fund-raising unless the leaders of the congregation are committed to these principles. Leadership casts the vision and mobilizes the congregation to action. At the top of this leadership team is the pastor of the congregation. If he is enthusiastic, excited, and committed to a positive course of action, it will generally happen. If he isn't, it usually won't. The pastor must be willing to step out and lead.

In the mid-1950s, I became the organizing pastor for the Village Community Presbyterian Church in

Rancho Santa Fe, California. We had no church property, buildings, or money. We had a wonderful group of people in a beautiful community who wanted a church. Our congregation was under the direction of a presbytery. In those days we could generally acquire land and erect the first unit, an all-purpose building, for about ninety thousand dollars. Those funds were developed as follows:

1. Thirty thousand dollars from a denominational, long-term, interest-free loan.
2. Thirty thousand dollars from a line of credit the presbytery had with the bank. The new congregation was expected to service this loan.
3. Thirty thousand dollars in cash that the local congregation would raise before anything could start.

Our official board had agreed to conduct a capital campaign to raise our thirty thousand. We had engaged a fund-raising firm to help us raise the money. But then the national economy went into a slump, and we had a recession. I remember the board meeting very well. It was held in my home. As moderator I called for a report of the capital campaign committee. The chairman, without my prior knowledge, simply announced that due to the economy, the capital campaign was called off. I had gone there to build a church. The community wanted a church. The only way we could start was to raise our local funds. I was dismayed. Something had to be done—right then. I felt all alone, but I asked the board if I could have a month to share the story of our need with the people and see if I could "prime the pump." They gave me permission to do anything I wanted but ordered me to call the professional campaign group and cancel our agreement. That night, after the meeting was adjourned and the board members had left, I wrote down twelve names of people in the congregation who I would personally visit and ask for a five-thousand-dollar commitment within thirty days. Remember, the board had said that we couldn't possibly raise any money because of the national economy.

I went to each of the twelve families with my message and my Bible. I began each visit by reading the familiar passage from Ecclesiastes 3, beginning with the words, "For everything there is a season. . . ." I read through the first eight verses and said, "I'm here because this is our season. We must raise the money to buy the land and erect a building or the window of opportunity may be gone." The people responded. When I reported to the board one month later, we had more money committed than our local share of the package required to proceed. Most of the commitments had come from the very board members who said, "We can't raise anything because of the economy." We continued to conduct our own local appeal and were able to acquire the land and dedicate the church debt free. Today that is a strong congregation with a far-reaching ministry.

It took pastoral leadership to make it happen. I had to take that position, and God gave me the strength, wisdom, grace, and zeal to fill the role.

That campaign, long before I had any professional training, may be the most satisfying fund-raising experience I have had in all these years in this career. I had to give leadership, and I did. That experience set the tone, the absolute golden maxim for fund-raising: *It is God who really makes it happen.*

God Gives the Increase

Throughout all these years, I have seen congregations raise millions of dollars for churches' needs. Each time,

I have been impressed with how the principles work and how good people have worked hard to raise the money. But what has impressed me the most is that God gives the increase. It has amazed me how often it appeared as though an appeal could not succeed, when suddenly (sometimes it seemed out of nowhere), the funds were secured and the mission was accomplished. No other answer is possible than that God willed it to happen.

Many experiences from actual fund-raising causes corroborate this conclusion. Perhaps one of the most vivid experiences for me was what happened at the Crystal Cathedral when we set out to erect the much needed family life center and offices for *Hour of Power*. We had tried to build it on our existing campus. We could not get the necessary building permits, and the site was not really adequate. So:

- We borrowed money to buy the five-acre parcel needed.
- We borrowed money to remove the fifty fourplexes that were on the property.
- We borrowed money to engage an architect.
- We borrowed money to hire a contractor.
- We started the project that would cost $26 million. We had five $1 million commitments and some money from the capital-funds appeal to the congregation. That was it.
- We were short a lot of money.

As Dr. Schuller said in his autobiography, *My Journey*, "Every night I had awakened at three in the morning, painfully exercising possibility thinking. Where would the money come from? Night after night I battled the temptation to meet with the architect and tell him to forget style and substance and just design a structure as inexpensive as possible."[1] I remember those times and the anguish of the challenge.

Suddenly things began to happen, as though another force had taken charge.

1. Dr. Schuller and his congregation had wisely purchased a parcel of land years before, but we couldn't sell it. Suddenly we had a buyer come to us when all the brokers had not succeeded. The buyer paid the full amount for the property.
2. The existing *Hour of Power* building across the street from the church property, and connected by a bridge over the street, had been on the market with several brokers and no success. Out of nowhere a neighbor came to us and offered full price for the building.
3. A magnificent estate in Maui, given to the ministry several years before, had been for sale for a long time, with no real prospects. Amazingly, a buyer appeared and offered us more than we had been asking for the property.

With these sales, and a few more special gifts, we were about to completely finish and furnish the entire project, and Dr. Schuller began to sleep better. It was obvious that God had given the increase. I have seen this happen so many times in church fund-raising that I have come to totally believe that if the need is real, the cause is right, and we work hard to implement tested fund-raising principles, somehow God will intervene and we will achieve our (his) purpose.

It takes faith, courage, dedication, and hard work. When it is all done, we can only say, "To God be the glory, great things he has done!"

NOTES

Chapter 1: *What Makes People Give?*

    1. Walt Kallestad, *Turn Your Church Inside Out* (Minneapolis: Augsburg/Fortress Press, 2001), 9.

Chapter 5: *Raising Funds for the Annual Budget*

    1. George Barna, *How to Increase Giving in Your Church* (Ventura, Calif.: Regal, 1997), 92–93.

Chapter 6: *Meeting the Challenges of a Growing Church*

    1. Jess Moody, lecture to theology students on church growth.

Chapter 8: *Stewardship in Perpetuity*

    1. Douglas K. Freeman, *Guidebook to Donors of Charitable Remainder Trusts*, copyright 2000 by Douglas K. Freeman, JP, LLM.

Epilogue

    1. Robert H. Schuller, *My Journey: From an Iowa Farm to a Cathedral of Dreams* (New York: HarperCollins, 2001), 273–74.

Chester L. Tolson, a fund-raising professional for nearly forty years, has played key development roles with organizations such as the Crystal Cathedral, the Presbyterian church, and Trinity University of San Antonio, Texas. For many years he has headed his own fundraising group. He has served as a senior pastor in California and Oregon and for the past six years has been the executive director of Churches Uniting in Global Mission, a network of senior pastors from the largest congregations in America. Tolson lives in Apple Valley, California.

For more information, visit the author's web site:
http://www.tolsongroup.com